SEAPOWER

SEAPOWER

JOHN GRESHAM
& IAN WESTWELL

CHARTWELL
BOOKS, INC.

This edition published by

CHARTWELL BOOKS, INC.
A Division of
BOOK SALES, INC.
114 Northfield Avenue
Edison, New Jersey 08837

ISBN-13: 978-0-7858-2462-6
ISBN-10: 0-7858-2462-6

Printed and bound in China

Design: Tony Stocks@Compendium

THE PHOTOGRAPHS

All the photo research for this book was undertaken by John
D. Gresham, with the able assistance of Melinda K. Day.
However, the photos in this book are unique in that all were
taken by military combat photographers, most on active duty
with the Navy or Marine Corps. Far from the "official" view
of naval and amphibious operations, the photos you see here
are how these military photojournalists see the world in which
they work and live. In doing so, they give those of us who
never will spend time on an aircraft carrier or submarine a
chance to see, often with emotion and drama, the exciting and
often dangerous world that is maritime and expeditionary
operations at the dawn of the 21st century. Far from simply
being "embedded" for a few weeks or months, like civilian
journalists during the recent war in Iraq, military combat
photographers are there 24/7, frequently as part of a ship's
crew or embarked Marine element. This is the world that they
live in, work in, and often these days, go to combat in. So
please, take a note of the names in each photo caption, for
there you will likely find future Pulitzer Prize winners, doing
their early work as combat photojournalists.

   As good as the photographers are, their work would go
unnoticed if there was not a distribution outlet for their work.
Thankfully, the U.S. Navy has invested in a world-class facility
and staff to accomplish this critical task. Located in the
Pentagon as part of the Navy's Information Office, is the
Navy Visual Media Center, run by Chris Madden. Chris and
his staff have tens of thousands of photos like the ones you
see here, digitized and ready to be delivered, downloaded, or
emailed to users around the world. These range from daily
newspapers to children doing reports for school. The best of
the collection is maintained on the U.S. Navy's official web
site, and can be accessed free of charge at
http://www.navy.mil, where anyone with some time and an
interest can see the daily "take" Chris and his team receive
from around the globe. It's an exciting place, and we would
like to thank them for our continued access to their facility to
select the photos you see here.

PAGE 1: USS *Dwight D. Eisenhower* (CVN 69). See page 74.
U.S. Navy photo by Photographer's Mate 3rd Class David E. Carter II

PAGE 2: The nuclear-powered aircraft carrier *USS Dwight D.
Eisenhower* (CVN 69) eases away from the pier in Mayport, Florida,
after a brief stop to pick up 1,200 family members (known as "tigers"
for a "Tiger Cruise") as the aircraft carrier completes the last two
days of a six-month overseas deployment.
U.S. Navy photo by Photographer's Mate 2nd Class David E. Carter II

RIGHT: Sailors man the rails while USS *Carl Vinson* (CVN 70) arrives
at Naval Air Station North Island, California to offload personnel
and equipment, before returning to her homeport at Naval Station
Bremerton, Washington, after an eight-month deployment to the
western Pacific.
U.S. Navy photo by Photographer's Mate 3rd Class Martin S. Fuentes

Contents

Introduction

The history of the U.S. Navy stretches back to the War of Independence, when some delegates to the Continental Congress suggested the creation of a colonial fleet to combat Britain's mighty Royal Navy. It was an idea that enjoyed the backing of George Washington but infuriated others, one of whom remarked that it was "the maddest idea in the world." Congress did agree to furnish and build warships and these served with distinction against the British, but the navy was all but abandoned after independence was won. A pattern of expansion and contraction was thus established that lasted until the end of World War II.

In the nineteenth century the navy grew to combat Barbary pirates in North Africa, fought the British in the War of 1812, took part in a host of small wars, fought to preserve the Union during the Civil War, and led the way for United States' expansion into the Pacific, but after each victory it was greatly reduced. Similar events followed during and after World War I. Although the conflict definitively established the United States as a leading maritime power, when World War II dawned the navy had to be greatly expanded to take part in the campaigns in the Pacific and Europe.

After World War II the navy was again reduced, but foreign policy soon changed dramatically due to the advent of the Cold War. Rather than withdrawing into isolationism as had previously been the case, henceforth the country would maintain a worldwide maritime role, chiefly to allow United States' shipping unhindered access to the world's seaways, to protect United States' overseas interests, and to curb the apparent expansionist threats posed by the Soviet Union and its satellite and client states. Thus the U.S. Navy had a concrete and worldwide role that demanded a large force, ultimately the largest in the world, although it remained (and remains) dogged by questions over finance.

The end of the Cold War in the late 1980s and early 1990s raised many new questions regarding the roles and tasks that the navy night be expected to perform.

The danger of superpower global conflict has ebbed away but has been replaced by numerous regional wars, many of which flare suddenly and threaten United States' strategic interests. Most recently, international terrorism has imperiled security both at home and abroad. The U.S. Navy was equipped to deter or fight the Soviet Union and its war strategy was directed toward battle against a rival maritime superpower. The resulting force strength and tactics do not conform to the requirements of regional conflicts and terrorism. New threats demand new strategies and new weapons that are still matters of debate.

The current buzzword is "asymmetrical" warfare, which means facing an unconventional enemy that will fight in unconventional and unexpected ways. Although the navy continues to see submarines, carriers, and amphibious forces as the cornerstones of its strength, increasingly greater resources will be funneled into developing greater special forces' capabilities and more multi-roled warships. Since World War II the navy has had a technological edge over any enemy and frequently greater firepower, yet while these facts remain true, planners are increasingly wrestling with the matters of flexibility, scale, and speed of the response to any crisis.

Aside from its strategic role—the deterrent provided by its nuclear-powered ballistic missile submarines—the cutting edge of the U.S. Navy, which is effectively split between the Atlantic and Pacific fleets, is its conventional forces that are based on three elements: first, attack submarines, both nuclear and conventional, tasked with maintaining free access to the world's oceans, protecting surface battle groups, and in some cases supporting land operations by deploying special forces and cruise missiles; second, carrier strike groups (CSGs); and third, amphibious ready groups (ARGs).

The CSGs and ARGs are the most visible assets deployed by the navy. The CSGs can be of variable size but revolve around a large carrier (the navy maintains twelve) with its multi-role air wing, which is supported by a range of smaller warships, typically:

- two guided-missile cruisers
- a guided-missile destroyer
- a destroyer and a frigate for anti-submarine work
- two attack submarines
- a combined ammunition, oiler, and supply ship

The CSGs, which are effectively a development of the carrier groups seen during World War II, are configured to protect U.S. military and commercial interests worldwide as dictated by the government; to neutralize enemy assets at sea, on land, and in the air in time of war; and to support ground operations by both Marine and army expeditionary forces. CSGs are currently evolving, particularly in relation to their surface ships; as new classes of cruiser and destroyers enter service they will take on more roles.

ABOVE: A CH-46 Sea Knight helicopter attached to the fast combat support ship USS *Bridge* (AOE 10) transfers supplies to the guided missile cruiser USS *Chosin* (CG 65) during a VERTREP. *Chosin* was on deployment in support of Operation Iraqi Freedom.
U.S. Navy photo by Photographer's Mate 1st Class Kevin H. Tierney

RIGHT: USS *Sacramento* (AOE 1) transfers jet fuel to USS *Carl Vinson* (CVN 70) during an RAS. *Sacramento* was part of the *Carl Vinson* CVBG providing logistics support during Operation Enduring Freedom.
U.S. Navy photo by Photographer's Mate Airman Inez Lawson

ARGs combine warships and ground forces, usually Marines but also army units. Typically they include a range of large amphibious assault vessels (AAVs) fitted with flightdecks and docking wells. These AAVs carry the troops to their objectives and then put them ashore using amphibious vehicles, landing craft, and helicopters. AGF task forces can also provide the troops with a measure of air support, typically AV-8B Harrier attack jets and AH-1W Super Cobra helicopter gunships, although carrier air wings—with their F/A-18 Hornets and F-14 Tomcats—are usually on hand to beef up the air component.

As well as these major classes of warship, the U.S. Navy also has a plethora of support craft to crew and maintain, including minesweepers, patrol craft, logistic vessels, and command ships. Aside from these smaller types, the navy operates around 300 major units at the present time. Yet even these might not be able to satisfy all of the United States' maritime needs in the coming decades, as not all the vessels can be deployed at any one time. In the early 1990s, for example, an average of 21 percent of the navy was deployed on operations at any given moment but by 2001 this had risen to 30 percent and, in an uncertain world, it is not beyond belief that this figure might rise further. As warships require repair and modernization, and their crews need rest and training, this trend, if it continues, might place intolerable strains on the service. The simple answer is to build more ships and find more sailors, yet the government does not have a bottomless purse and, equally, evidence suggests it may struggle to find new men and women—at the time of writing it is short of some 14,000 recruits. The future of the modern navy, as it has been in the past, remains uncertain.

FAR LEFT: An underway stern view of the USS *Dwight D. Eisenhower* (CVN 69). Just below the flightdeck on the fantail are a Mk. 15 Phalanx 20mm CIWS and the ship's jet engine test stand.
U.S. Navy photo

LEFT: An F/A-18 Hornet of VFA-151 (the "Vigilantes") launches from USS *Constellation* (CV 64) as the guided-missile cruiser USS *Mobile Bay* (CG 53) steams alongside.
U.S. Navy photo by Photographer's Mate 2nd Class Felix Garza Jr.

Aircraft Carriers

Carriers form the heart of the U.S. Navy and at present the country's twelve-strong carrier force is based around the nuclear-powered aircraft carriers (CVNs) of the nine-ship (to date) Nimitz class and the single ship of the Enterprise class, and the two conventionally powered aircraft carriers (CVs) of the single-ship Kitty Hawk and John F. Kennedy classes. The vessels each form the heart of a carrier battle group (CVBG), which also includes escorts and replenishment vessels. Their primary role is to act as what is termed a "forward presence". This means that they provide a credible, sustainable, and conventional deterrence against potential aggressors in peacetime and then in time of war form the core of any U.S. overseas expeditionary force. Operationally, the carriers deploy their air wings to either act independently against any air, water, or land threats that could prevent the unhindered use of the world's seaways or act in tandem with ground operations .

LEFT: The aircraft carrier *USS Carl Vinson* (CVN 70) enters the channel into Pearl Harbor for a liberty visit after completing a deployment in support of Operation Enduring Freedom.
U.S. Navy Photo by Chief Photographer's Mate Daniel E. Smith

OPPOSITE, ABOVE: An F/A-18 Hornet launches from the flight-deck of the aircraft carrier *USS Kitty Hawk* (CV 63) while operating in the Western Pacific Ocean.
U.S. Navy photo by Photographer's Mate 3rd Class Alex C. Witte

OPPOSITE, BELOW: Ordnance personnel aboard the aircraft carrier *USS Kitty Hawk* (CV-63) prepare a target banner to be towed by an F-14A Tomcat from the "Black Knights" of Fighter Squadron VF-154. The banner is used for target practice by F/A-18C Hornets and F-14A Tomcats.
U.S. Navy photo by Photographer's Mate 1st Class William R. Goodwin

Enterprise Class

BELOW: Shouldering an aircraft holdback bar, an aviation boatswain's mate stands by a steaming catapult as it is prepared for launching another aircraft. The carrier—USS *Enterprise*—was operating in the Atlantic Ocean at the time.
U.S. Navy photo by Photographer's Mate 2nd Class Marlow P. Dix

RIGHT: The flightdeck of the USS *Enterprise* is crammed with aircraft while underway in the Arabian Gulf.
U.S. Navy photo by Photographer's Mate 3rd Class Douglas Pearlman

The *Enterprise* (CVN 65) was the U.S. Navy's first nuclear-powered carrier and its origins date back to the early 1950s when work was begun on the design of suitable powerplants. To the alarm of some, the cost of the *Enterprise*'s new propulsion system was extremely high and made the vessel almost twice as expensive to build in comparison to the similar but conventionally powered Kitty Hawk class of carriers. Nevertheless, others argued that in the long term nuclear power meant that the carrier required refueling less frequently and could therefore remain on station for greater periods. Equally, there was no longer any need to load huge quantities of bulky fuel for its propulsion system and so the *Enterprise* could carry up to 50 percent more aviation fuel for its aircraft, thus allowing them to stay operational for longer.

Built by Newport News Shipbuilding in just three years and nine months, *Enterprise* was deployed for service on November 25, 1961. In looks the carrier was much like the Kitty Hawks, although its superstructure was much more box like; this was totally removed during a refit between 1979 and 1981 and replaced by a new central island similar to that seen on the Nimitz class. The *Enterprise* was originally deployed in the Atlantic but was transferred to the Pacific along with her escorts for service in the Vietnam War and remained on station there long after the conflict ended. The carrier's home base is now Norfolk, Virginia. Although discussions were held to add another unit to the Enterprise class in the early 1960s, they were shelved due to financial constraints.

Length: 1,123 feet
Displacement: 89,600 tons (full load)
Flightdeck: 252 feet (width); 1,088 feet (length)
Speed: 30+ knots
Crew: 3,350 (ship's company); 2,480 (air wing)
Armament: Two NATO Sea Sparrow SAM launchers; two Phalanx CIWSs
Aircraft: 85

LEFT: USSs *Enterprise* (above—CVN 65) and *Carl Vinson* (below—CVN 70) meet briefly in the waters of the Arabian Gulf following the 9/11 terrorist attacks. *U.S. Navy photo by Photographer's Mate Third Class Douglas M. Pearlman*

BELOW: The flightdeck of USS *Enterprise* (CVN 65) becomes a stage as country and western singer Garth Brooks performs for the *Enterprise* CVBG sailors and families during a coast-to-coast television broadcast.
U.S. Navy photo by Photographer's Mate 2nd Class William R. Crosby

BELOW: A crew member performs maintenance on an aircraft on USS *Enterprise*.
U.S. Navy photo by Photographer's Mate 2nd Class Vladimir Garcia

ABOVE: USS *Enterprise* steams alongside the fast combat support ship USS *Arctic* (AOE 8) while conducting a VERTREP in the Arabian Gulf.
U.S. Navy photo by Photographer's Mate Third Class Douglas M. Pearlman

RIGHT: An F-14A Tomcat taxis to catapult number one for launch from USS *Enterprise* (CVN 65).
U.S. Navy photo by Photographer's Mate 2nd Class Darryl I. Wood

FAR RIGHT: Two naval aviators converse on the flightdeck of USS *Enterprise*.
U.S. Navy photo by Photographer's Mate 2nd Class Darryl I. Wood

FOLLOWING PAGES (18/19):
PAGE 18: The fast combat support ship USS *Arctic* (AOE 8) pulls alongside USS *Enterprise* for an underway RAS, while the destroyer USS *Nicholson* (DD 982) follows.
U.S. Navy photo by Photographer's Mate 3rd Class Douglas M. Pearlman.

PAGE 19: Aviation ordnancemen of USS *Enterprise's* "Sidewinders"—VFA-86— remove a hoisting sling from an ammo crate carrying 2,000 lb Mk. 84 general purpose bombs.
U.S. Navy photo by Photographer's Mate 3rd Class Lance H. Mayhew, Jr.

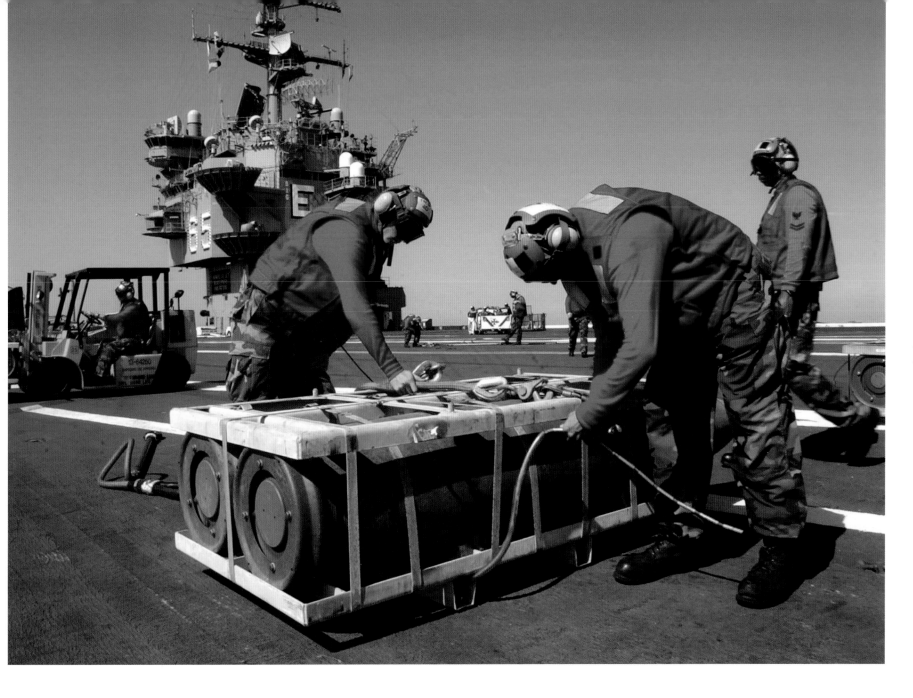

ABOVE: Preparing ammo on the flightdeck of USS *Dwight D. Eisenhower* (CVN 69) to be offloaded to USS *Enterprise* (CVN 65). *Eisenhower* was operating in the Atlantic Ocean on an ammunition offload and flightdeck certification.
U.S. Navy photo by Photographer's Mate 3rd Class Josh Treadwell

RIGHT: USS *Enterprise* en route to its homeport following an extended deployment that included missions in support of Operation Enduring Freedom.
U.S. Navy photo by Photographer's Mate 3rd Class Douglas M. Pearlman

BELOW: USS *Enterprise* (CVN 65) conducts a port turn after an emergency break away drill with MSC fast combat support ship USNS *Leroy Grumman* (T-AO 195) off the Atlantic coast.
U.S. Navy photo by Photographer's Mate 2nd Class Douglas M. Pearlman

RIGHT: USS *Enterprise* steams alongside USNS *Leroy Grumman* during a replenishment while underway during carrier qualifications.
U.S. Navy photo by Photographer's Mate 2nd Class Douglas M. Pearlman

LEFT: The aircraft carrier USS *Independence* (CV 62) refuels from MSC oiler USNS *Walter S. Diehl* (T-AO 193) while forward-deployed to the Persian Gulf.
U. S. Navy photo by Photographer's Mate Airman Chris Howell

INSET LEFT: An aviation boatswain's mate (known as a "plane handler") directs an E-2C Hawkeye to the catapult on the flight deck of the nuclear-powered aircraft carrier USS *Enterprise* (CVN 65).
U.S. Navy photo by Photographer's Mate 3rd Class David Pastoriza

RIGHT: An E-2C Hawkeye from Airborne Early Warning Squadron VAW-124 (the "Bear Aces") makes an arrested landing on the flightdeck of nuclear-powered aircraft carrier USS *Enterprise* (CVN 65).
U. S. Navy Photo by Photographer's Mate 2nd Class Darryl I Wood

FAR LEFT: The nuclear-powered aircraft carrier USS *Enterprise* (CVN 65) begins a morning transit north through the Suez Canal to the Mediterranean Sea.
U.S. Navy photo by Photographer's Mate 2nd Class Darryl I. Wood

LEFT: A CH-46 Sea Knight "crossdecks" a jet engine and trailer between USS *Enterprise* and USS *Carl Vinson* (CVN 70).
U.S. Navy photo by Photographer's Mate 3rd Class Jeremy Kerns

LEFT: Aviation Warfare Specialist Charles C. Duke and Aviation Boatswain's Mate First Class Hector M. Arroyo prepare equipment for an aircraft salvage drill during a general quarters exercise on board USS *Enterprise*.
U.S. Navy photo by Photographer's Mate Third Class Lance H. Mayhew Jr..

RIGHT: USS *Enterprise* in the Atlantic Ocean while preparing for a deployment to the Mediterranean. CVBGs spend six months preparing for such deployments, which are made in concert with amphibious ready groups, and Marine expeditionary units.
U.S. Navy photo by Photographer's Mate 2nd Class Douglas M. Pearlman

RIGHT: Sailors aboard USS *Enterprise* (CVN 65) remove the barrel of a .50-caliber machine gun during a live-fire exercise while underway in the Atlantic Ocean. Every U.S. Navy vessel is equipped with small-bore weapons to help protect against threats from small boats, light aircraft, and swimmers. *U.S. Navy photo by Photographer's Mate Airman Rob Gaston*

FAR RIGHT: Members of the deck department on board USS *Enterprise* await a pallet of supplies during an underway replenishment and refueling with the fast combat support ship USS *Detroit* (AOE 4). *U.S. Navy photo by Photographer's Mate 1st Class Nicholas D. Sherrouse*

John F. Kennedy Class

The *John F. Kennedy* (CV 67) was originally planned as the fourth unit of the Kitty Hawk class, but in 1963 the navy requested that the new vessel be nuclear-powered. However, Congress became alarmed at the potential construction budget and, as a cost-saving measure, the *Kennedy* was fitted with the same eight boilers and four steam turbines that were standard in the Kitty Hawk class. Its flightdeck arrangement was also generally the same as these carriers, but the *Kennedy* had some noticeably different external features, particularly a new type of canted smokestack, which was designed to blow corrosive exhaust gases away from the flightdeck, and a different shape to the end of the forward deck. More significantly it was the first carrier to be fitted with a basic point defense missile system (BPDMS), which replaced the more expensive long-range Terrier area defense systems seen on other Kitty Hawks that effectively did no more than duplicate similar systems found on carrier escort warships. Construction work was given to Newport News Shipbuilding of Virginia in 1964 and the carrier was deployed for service on September 7, 1968. When the *Kennedy* was launched it set a new bench mark for U.S. carrier design and the subsequent Nimitz class of nuclear-powered vessels are remarkably similar in the arrangement of their weapons systems, sensors, and flightdeck. The weapons systems in the other carriers in the Kitty Hawk class were all subsequently upgraded to the same standard as the *Kennedy*. The carrier, a single-ship class, mostly serves in the Atlantic, with frequent visits to the Mediterranean, and its home port is Mayport, Florida.

Length: 1,052 feet
Displacement: 82,000 tons (full load)
Flightdeck: 252 feet (width); 1046 feet (length)
Speed: 30+ knots
Crew: 3,117 (ship's company); 2,480 (air wing)
Armament: NATO Sea Sparrow SAMs with box launchers; two Phalanx CIWSs
Aircraft: 85

LEFT: The U.S. Navy's Blue Angels flight demonstration team fly by the island structure of the USS *John F. Kennedy* (CV 67).
U.S. Navy photo by Photographer's Mate 2nd Class Grant Goods

RIGHT: An HH-60H Seahawk helicopter assigned to Helicopter Anti-Submarine Squadron HS-5—the "Nightdippers"—crosses the bow of USS *John F. Kennedy*, as it enters the Mediterranean Sea to support Operation Enduring Freedom.
U.S. Navy photo by Photographer's Mate 1st Class Jim Hampshire

FOLLOWING PAGES (34/35):
PAGE 34: USS *John F. Kennedy* passes through Chesapeake Bay as the ship approaches the naval station in Norfolk, Virginia, prior to disembarking part of her air wing personnel. The *Kennedy* would then continue the final leg of a six-month deployment to Mayport, Florida, where the ship is homeported.
U.S. Navy photo by Photographer's Mate 1st Class Martin Maddock

PAGE 35: An SH-60 Seahawk attached to HS-3 flies plane guard duty near USS *John F. Kennedy*.
U.S. Navy photo by Photographer's Mate 2nd Class Scott A. Moak

LEFT: In honor of the new century, the crew of USS *John F. Kennedy* (CV 67) stands in formation to spell out "2000" on the aircraft carrier's flightdeck while in the Arabian Gulf in support of Operation Southern Watch.
U.S. Navy photo by Photographer's Mate 2nd Class Christian S. Eskelund

ABOVE: Crewmembers of USS *John F. Kennedy* man the rails as it pulls into Marmaris, Turkey, having conducted combat missions in support of Operation Enduring Freedom. The *Kennedy* was relieved by the USS *George Washington* (CVN 73) CVBG.
U.S. Navy photo by Photographer's Mate 1st Class Jim Hampshire

LEFT: Crewmen man the rails as the USS *John F. Kennedy* (CV 67) passes under the Verrazano Narrows suspension bridge between Staten Island and Brooklyn, New York, as the ship navigates up the Hudson River to New York City to participate in International Naval Review 2000.

U. S. Navy photo by Photographer's Mate 1st Class Tina M. Ackerman

ABOVE: USS *John F. Kennedy* (left) and the decommissioned aircraft carrier USS *Intrepid* (right) flank a group of international tall ships while docked in New York City during International Naval Review 2000.

U.S. Navy photo by Photographer's Mate 1st Class Jim Hampshire

Kitty Hawk Class

The name ship of the class, the USS *Kitty Hawk* (CV 63), was built by the New York Ship Building Corporation of Camden, New Jersey, and deployed for service on April 29, 1961, making it the oldest unit of the U.S. Navy's current carrier force. The *Kitty Hawk* was envisaged as a update of the ageing Forrestal class, which had been built between 1952 and 1955, and among the most significant changes were the increase of the flightdeck area and the repositioning of the single port side aircraft lift, which was located forward on the Forrestal class. This was moved aft, so that it can still be used when aircraft are landing. On the starboard side the second central lift and island superstructure had their positions reversed so that this lift could also deploy aircraft to the forward catapults. This arrangement of lifts and superstructure proved so successful that the layout was adopted for all subsequent U.S. carriers. The new class was also the first to incorporate surface-to-air missiles for air defense and the last to be powered by gas turbines—eight boilers drive four steam turbines that power four shafts. All of the carriers were built between 1961 and 1968 and four were launched. Aside from the *Kitty Hawk*, these were the *Constellation* (CV 64), the *America* (CV 66), and the *John F. Kennedy* (CV 67), although the latter is officially considered a separate, single-ship class. *Constellation* and *America* have been decommissioned. *Kitty Hawk* is still operational from its home base of Yokosuka, Japan.

Length: 1,062.5 feet
Displacement: 80,800 tons (full load)
Flightdeck: 252 feet (width); 1,046 feet (length)
Speed: 30+ knots
Crew: 3,150 (ship's company); 2,480 (air wing)
Armament: NATO Sea Sparrow SAM launchers; three Phalanx CIWSs
Aircraft: 85

LEFT: USS *Kitty Hawk* (CV 63) steams under a full moon while conducting flight operations in the Gulf of Thailand.
U.S. Navy photo by Photographer's Mate 2nd Class Keith Bryska

RIGHT: USS *Kitty Hawk* tied up at Echo Wharf pier in Guam before getting underway the next morning for a scheduled deployment. The *Kitty Hawk* celebrated its fortieth anniversary while at Guam. It is named after the small North Carolina town near Orville and Wilbur Wright's first manned flight of 1903.
U.S. Navy photo by Photographer's Mate 2nd Class Alan D. Monyelle

LT PAUL RIEHLE
RUFUS

CDR HAROLD BISHOP
COMMANDING OFFICER
BUD

501

AN FRANK
"OILBERT"
MUNCIE, IN

DANCEJ

C02   AFFF

LEFT: Aviation Boatswain's Mate Airman Roy Diaz hooks a launch bar to an EA-6B Prowler assigned to the "Gauntlets," USS *Kitty Hawk*'s Electronic Attack Squadron VAQ-136, during catapult launch preparations.
U. S. Navy photo by Photographer's Mate 1st Class William R. Goodwin

RIGHT: USS *Kitty Hawk* (CV 63) is seen head-on at high speed during a transit to her home-port of Yokosuka, Japan, while returning after a six-month deployment to the Arabian Gulf.
U.S. Navy photo by Chief Photographer's Mate Mahlon K. Miller

LEFT: USS *Kitty Hawk* (CV 63) departs Thailand after a scheduled port visit.
U.S. Navy photo by Photographer's Mate Airman Apprentice Lee McCaskill

FAR LEFT: Aboard USS *Kitty Hawk* (CV 63) October 16, 2003 - A C-2A Greyhound assigned to the "Providers" of Fleet Logistics Squadron VRC-30 lines up to be launched from USS *Kitty Hawk* (CV 63). The aircraft carrier recently completed an extensive five-month maintenance period in Yokosuka, Japan.
U.S. Navy photo by Photographer's Mate 3rd Class Jason T. Poplin.

LEFT: USS *Kitty Hawk* (CV 63) sails past Mount Fuji while getting underway for a deployment in the western Pacific.
U.S. Navy photo by Photographer's Mate 3rd Class John Sullivan

ABOVE: Tugboats assist USS *Kitty Hawk* to get underway to conduct sea trials after completing a successful five-month overhaul in Yokosuka, Japan.
U.S. Navy photo by Photographer's Mate 1st Class Warner

Nimitz Class

The ships of the Nimitz class are the second generation of U.S. nuclear-powered carriers and reflect lessons learned from their sole predecessor, the *Enterprise*. Unlike the latter's eight reactors that each generate 35,000 shaft horsepower, the Nimitz class ships are powered by just two, more advanced, reactors that each generate 130,000 shaft horsepower. The uranium cores used in these more modern and efficient powerplants also require replacing less frequently—just one every thirteen years—and take up considerably less space, thereby allowing the Nimitz vessels to carry 20 percent more aviation fuel, munitions, and other stores. The name ship of the class, the USS *Nimitz* (CVN 68), was built by Newport News Shipbuilding and was deployed on May 3, 1975. However, the carrier had been dogged by numerous problems. From the outset there was a short-age of skilled labor and the dockyard was hit by several strikes. Consequently, the *Nimitz*, which had already been ordered four years later than intended, took seven years to build. Even when the construction work was completed in 1973, it took a further two years to finish the installation of her reactors. Such delays impacted on the delivery of later vessels in the class and the spiraling costs prompted President Jimmy Carter to attempt to block delivery of a fourth vessel and replace the design with a cheaper one that was unpopular with the U.S. Navy. Carter failed and his successor, Ronald Reagan, gave the go-ahead for further ships. The nine Nimitz carriers now in service are based at San Diego, California (3), Newport News (1) and Norfolk (3), Virginia, and Bremerton (1) and Everett (1), Washington. The keel of the tenth ship in the class, the *George H. W. Bush*, was laid down on September 6, 2003.

Length: 1,040 feet

Displacement: 97,000 tons (full load)

Flightdeck: 252 feet (width); 1,092 feet (length)

Speed: 30+ knots

Crew: 3,200 (ship's company); 2,480 (air wing)

Armament: Two or three NATO Sea Sparrow SAM launchers; three or four Phalanx CIWSs (three on USSs *Nimitz* and *Dwight D. Eisenhower* and four on subsequent units)

Aircraft: 85

LEFT: A maintenance crew attached to the "Argonauts"—Strike Fighter Squadron VFA-147—conducts instrument tests on an F/A-18C Hornet aboard the aircraft carrier USS *Carl Vinson* (CVN 70), while participating in an annual joint exercise known as "Foal Eagle" in the Sea of Japan.
U.S. Navy photo by Photographer's Mate 2nd Class Nathan L. Guimont

RIGHT: Aviation ordnancemen attach cargo netting and hooks to barrels for movement by helicopter to a supply ship from USS *Abraham Lincoln* (CVN 72) during Operation Iraqi Freedom.
U.S. Navy photo by Photographer's Mate Airman Bernardo Fuller

LEFT: A plane captain aboard USS *Carl Vinson* (CVN 70) prepares an HH-60H Sea Hawk assigned to Helicopter Anti–Submarine Squadron HS-8— the "Eight Ballers"—for the next launch cycle of a regularly scheduled six-month deployment in the western Pacific Ocean.
U.S. Navy photo by Photographer's Mate 3rd Class Martin S. Fuentes

RIGHT: Munitions on USS *Abraham Lincoln* (CVN 70). The GPS-guided bombs are in temporary storage prior to being loaded onto aircraft during Operation Iraqi Freedom.
U.S. Navy photo by Photographer's Mate 3rd Class Michael S. Kelly

DANGER
AMMUNITION
HANDLING
KEEP OUT

FROM
G-3
WEAPONS
ASSEMBLY

FROM
G-3 WEAPONS
ASSEMBLY
MADE IN THE USA

RIGHT: USS *Ronald Reagan* (CVN 76), while still precommissioning and on builder's trials, passes the lighthouse at Fort Story Army Base, Virginia.
U.S. Navy photo Photographer's Mate 2nd Class Alisha M. Frederick

FAR RIGHT: Sailors aboard USS *Dwight D. Eisenhower* (CVN 69) gather on the flightdeck to spell out "IKE 2000," referring to their successful deployment to the Mediterranean Sea in the new millennium. Cruising with *Eisenhower* are the guided-missile cruisers USSs *Anzio* (CG 68) and *Cape St. George* (CG 71).
U.S. Navy photo by Photographer's Mate 2nd Class David E. Carter II

FOLLOWING PAGES (54/55):
MAIN PHOTO: Weatherbeaten from a nearly ten-month deployment in support of Operations Enduring Freedom and Iraqi Freedom, USS *Abraham Lincoln* (CVN 72) returns home to Everett, Washington.
U.S. Navy photo by Photographer's Mate 2nd Class Michael B. W. Watkins

PAGE 54 (INSET LEFT): A pair of S-3B Viking aircraft assigned to Sea Control Squadron VS-33 —the "Screwbirds"—and configured as airborne tankers are launched from the bow and waist catapults of USS *Carl Vinson*.
U.S. Navy photo by Photographer's Mate Airman Chris M. Valdez

PAGE 54 (INSET RIGHT): A pilot in his F/A-18C Hornet aboard USS *Abraham Lincoln* awaits his turn to be hooked up to one of the steam catapults and launched on a mission during Operation Iraqi Freedom.
U.S. Navy photo by Airman Jeanine Garcia

ABOVE: Explosive Ordnance Disposal and SEAL team personnel practice special insertion and extraction techniques from an SH-60 Seahawk above the aircraft carrier USS *Dwight D. Eisenhower* (CVN 69) while on a six-month deployment to the Mediterranean Sea.
U.S. Navy photo by Photographer's Mate 2nd Class Leland B. Comer

RIGHT: F-14 Tomcat and F/A-18 Hornet fighter-bombers fly over the newest Nimitz-class aircraft carrier, USS *Ronald Reagan* (CVN 76), at the conclusion of the commissioning ceremony for the ship.
U.S. Navy photo by Photographer's Mate 2nd Class Charles A. Edwards Jr.

FAR RIGHT: Steam rises from a waist catapult as an F/A-18C from Strike Fighter Squadron VFA-97 prepares for a launch from USS *Kitty Hawk* (CV 63) in the Arabian Gulf.
U.S. Navy photo by Chief Photographer's Mate Mahlon K. Miller

LEFT: The AEGIS guided missile destroyer USS *John Paul Jones* (DDG 53) pulls alongside the aircraft carrier USS *John C. Stennis* (CVN 74) for an underway RAS off the southern California coast.
U.S. Navy photo by Photographer's Mate 3rd Class Joshua Word

RIGHT: The view from the port-hole of a CH-46 Sea Knight helicopter assigned to Helicopter Combat Support Squadron HC-8—the "Dragon Whales"—as it delivers supplies to the flightdeck of USS *George Washington* (CVN 73).
U.S. Navy photo by Photographer's Mate 1st Class David C. Lloyd

BELOW: Vice Admiral Timothy J. Keating, Commander U.S. Naval Forces Fifth Fleet, lands on the flightdeck of USS *Nimitz* (CVN 68) in an F/A-18F Super Hornet from Strike Fighter Squadron VFA-41 while deployed in support of Operation Iraqi Freedom. The Super Hornet is the navy's newest fighter, replacing the ageing F-14 Tomcat and older versions of the F/A-18 Hornet.
U.S. Navy photo by Photographer's Mate 3rd Class Yesenia Rosas

RIGHT: USS *Harry S. Truman* (CVN 75) pulls away from pier 14, Naval Station Norfolk, to begin her transit to the Norfolk Navy Shipyard.
U. S. Navy photo by Photographer's Mate 2nd Class John L. Beeman

LEFT: Tug boats guide the aircraft carrier USS *Harry S. Truman* (CVN 75) up the Elizabeth River, past tourist hotels in Portsmouth, Virginia, to the Norfolk Naval Shipyard. Heavy use requires regular yard repair periods to keep America's warships ready for duty around the world.
U. S. Navy photo by Photographer's Mate 2nd Class John L. Beeman

RIGHT: An SH-60 Seahawk helicopter comes in for a landing aboard USS *Nimitz* (CVN 68) as the ship navigates the busy sea lanes in the Indian Ocean.
U.S. Navy photo by Photographer's Mate 2nd Class Monica L. McLaughlin

BELOW: A full moon illuminates the nuclear aircraft carrier USS *Carl Vinson* (CVN 70) during pre-deployment flight operations off the southern California coast.
U.S. Navy photo by Electronics Warfare Technician 2nd Class Christopher Ware

FOLLOWING PAGES (64/65):

PAGE 64: Under a lifting fog, USS *Carl Vinson* prepares to anchor outside Hong Kong Island for a scheduled liberty call while deployed in the western Pacific. Such deployments regularly last over six months, and take carrier battle groups to the Persian Gulf and other distant operating areas.
U.S. Navy photo by Photographer's Mate Third Class Martin S. Fuentes

PAGE 65 MAIN PICTURE: Backed by a beautiful Pacific sunset, F/A-18F Super Hornets from the "Diamondbacks" of Strike Fighter Squadron VFA-102 prepare for night flight operations aboard the flightdeck of USS *John C. Stennis* (CVN 74) while conducting training exercises off the Southern California coast.
U.S. Navy photo by Photographer's Mate Airman Mark J. Rebilas

PAGE 65 (INSET): Sailors assigned to Fighter Squadron VF-32—the "Swordsmen"—perform maintenance to an F-14 Tomcat in the hangar bay of USS *Harry S. Truman* while on deployment conducting missions in support of Operation Iraqi Freedom.
U.S. Navy photo by Photographer's Mate Airman Ryan O'Connor

LEFT: Sailors look for FOD—foreign object debris—on the angled flightdeck of USS *John C. Stennis* (CVN 74) while off the California coast. FOD walk downs are important in the prevention of damage to aircraft engines and injuries to flightdeck personnel.
U.S. Navy photo by Photographer's Mate Airman Mark J. Rebilas

FAR LEFT: Sunset at Mayport, Florida, highlights the aircraft carriers (foreground) USS *Dwight D. Eisenhower* (CVN 69) and (pierside) USS *John F. Kennedy* (CV 67). The *Eisenhower* was departing Mayport after picking up 1,200 family members and friends for a two-day "Tiger Cruise."
U.S. Navy photo by Photographer's Mate 2nd Class David E. Carter II

RIGHT: USS *Nimitz* (left, CVN 68) approaches her sister ship the USS *George Washington* (right—CVN 73), during operations in the Northern Arabian Gulf.
U.S. Navy photo by PH2 Matthew J. Magee

OPPOSITE PAGE, ABOVE LEFT: As an SH-60 Seahawk flies overwatch patrol, USS *John C. Stennis* (CVN 74) moves down the San Diego Harbor channel, as it heads to sea under a cloud of smoke from nearby fall wildfires.
U.S. Navy photo by Photographer's Mate Airman Mark Rebilas

OPPOSITE PAGE, BELOW LEFT: T-45 Goshawks line the flight-deck during refueling aboard USS *Dwight D. Eisenhower* (CVN 69). The T-45 is used to train Naval Aviators during initial carrier qualifications.
U.S. Navy photo by Photographer's Mate Airman James P. Wagner

OPPOSITE PAGE, RIGHT: On the flightdeck of the USS *Nimitz* (CVN 68) CVW-11 aircraft are strategically parked during a scheduled no fly day. The Nimitz Strike Group was deployed in support of Operation Iraqi Freedom
U.S. Navy photo by Airman Angel G Hilbrands

ABOVE: An E-2C Hawkeye from Airborne Early Warning Squadron VAW-125—the "Tigertails"—and an EA-6B Prowler from Tactical Electronic Warfare Squadron VAQ-132—the "Scorpions"—stand ready on the flightdeck of USS *George Washington* (CVN 73) while taking part in Exercise Mediterranean Shark.
U.S. Navy photo by Photographer's Mate Airman Lindsay Switzer

RIGHT: USS *Carl Vinson* (CVN 70) arrives in her homeport of Bremerton, Washington after completing an extended deployment.
U.S. Navy photo

LEFT: Behind a threatening sky, Airmen from the Helicopter Anti-Submarine Squadron HS-8—the "Eightballers"—rush to chock and chain an SH-60F Sea Hawk aboard USS *Carl Vinson* (CVN 70) in preparation for a crew change. Flight operations continue around the clock, as air officers try to maximize the number of sorties in every day's air plan.
U.S. Navy photo by Photographer's Mate 2nd Class Inez Lawson

BELOW: Plane captain, Airman Corey Vandergriff from San Diego, California, observes flightdeck operations aboard USS *John C. Stennis* (CVN 74) during training exercises in the Southern California operating area.
U.S. Navy photo by Photographer's Mate Airman Mark J. Rebilas

LEFT: Signal flags fly from the flightdeck to the top of the island structure of USS *Theodore Roosevelt* (CVN 71) during a change of command ceremony for the Commander, U.S. Atlantic Fleet at Naval Station Norfolk, Virginia.
U.S. Navy photo by Photographer's Mate Airman Jacob Fadley

ABOVE: A T-45 Goshawk jet trainer launches from the flightdeck of USS *Dwight D. Eisenhower* (CVN 69) while underway in the Atlantic Ocean conducting carrier qualifications.
U.S. Navy photo by Photographer's Mate Airman James P. Wagner

LEFT: Sailors man the rails on the flightdeck of USS *John C. Stennis* (CVN 74) as the ship arrives in port for the annual San Diego Fleet Week parade of ships ceremony.
Photographer's Mate 3rd Class Joshua Word

FAR LEFT: USS *Dwight D. Eisenhower* cuts through the warm waters of the eastern Mediterranean while on a routine six-month deployment.
U.S. Navy photo by Photographer's Mate 3rd Class David E. Carter II

RIGHT: An F/A-18C Hornet from Strike Fighter Squadron VFA-136—the "Knighthawks" —roars down catapult number one and launches from the flightdeck of USS *Dwight D. Eisenhower* (CVN 69). *U.S. Navy photo by Photographer's Mate Third Class Josh Treadwell*

BELOW RIGHT: Early morning fog drifts across the flightdeck of the aircraft carrier USS *Carl Vinson* (CVN 70) before a underway replenishment period later that morning. *U.S. Navy photo by Photographer's Mate 3rd Class Martin S. Fuentes*

FAR RIGHT: Sailors assigned to the aircraft carrier USS *Dwight D. Eisenhower*, background, and guided-missile destroyers USSs *McFaul* (DDG 74—left), and *Ross* (DDG 71—right) attend a memorial service at Naval Station Norfolk, Virginia, along with family members and friends of sailors killed and missing as a result of the October 12, 2000, terrorist attack on USS *Cole* (DDG 67). *U.S. Navy photo by Photographer's Mate 2nd Class Robert McRill*

FAR LEFT: Crew members of the USS *John F. Kennedy* (CV 67) watch from the ship's hangar bay as the sun rises over USS *Theodore Roosevelt* (CVN 71).
U.S. Navy photo by Photographer's Mate 1st Class Jim Hampshire

LEFT: A GPS-guided AGM-154 joint stand-off weapon on the flightdeck of USS *Dwight D. Eisenhower* (CVN 69) during a routine deployment in the Mediterranean.
U.S. Navy photo by Photographer's Mate 2nd Class Leland B. Comer

BELOW LEFT: Captain Mark McNally, Commanding Officer of USS *Dwight D. Eisenhower*, sits in his captain's chair while watching flight operations in support of an ammunition offload/onload between *Eisenhower* and USS *Enterprise* (CVN 65) in the Atlantic Ocean.
U.S. Navy photo by Photographer's Mate Airman Angela Elizabeth Padilla

Cruisers

The *Ticonderoga* and its 26 sister warships, the U.S. Navy's only class of these large surface vessels, are designated guided-missile cruisers (CG) and are equipped to conduct a variety of roles, chiefly in relation to dealing with multiple air, surface, and underwater threats. Their multi-range radar arrays and integrated weapons systems allow them to perform a number of defensive maritime tasks including the protection of carrier battle groups and amphibious forces. They are also sufficiently versatile to act independently or as flagships for larger forces, and their ability to carry out long-range offensive tasks has been expanded by the addition of the Tomahawk cruise missile system.

RIGHT: The Aegis guided-missile cruiser USS *Normandy* (CG 60) leans starboard as it executes a high-speed turn while operating in the Mediterranean Sea.
U.S. Navy Photo by Photographer's Mate 2nd Class Shane McCoy

FAR RIGHT: Photographed from USS *Dwight D. Eisenhower* (CVN 69), the Ticonderoga-class cruiser *USS Cape St. George* (CG 71) sails off the Eastern Coast of the United States.
U.S. Navy photo by Photographer's Mate 3rd Class David E. Carter II

Ticonderoga Class

The first of the class, USS *Ticonderoga* (CG 47), was launched on January 22, 1983, and the 27 (CG 47–73) such cruisers that are in service at present were built by either Ingalls Shipbuilding or the Bath Iron Works. The class was the first in the U.S. Navy to be fitted with the integrated AEGIS combat system that was designed to track and neutralize multiple threats by integrating target-acquisition and weapon systems. It was intended that they would be deployed to carrier battle groups in pairs to deal with saturation missile attacks by Soviet forces. As multiple threats develop at various ranges and heights from sea level to the zenith, the ship's SPY-1 radar and combat system integrator can individually identify and track the numerous targets, evaluate and prioritize the danger posed by each, and then select the appropriate defensive system, although a manual over-ride is also available. The class's basic design originated in the budget-cutting 1970s and utilized the upgrade potential of the conventionally powered Spruance class of destroyers. The destroyer's basic hull and layout was enlarged to incorporate the AEGIS system's more complex electronics and a greater range of weapons system, rather than build a costly nuclear-powered warship from scratch as had been originally intended. At present the cruisers' home bases are in San Diego, California (7), Mayport, Florida (4) , Pearl Harbor, Hawaii (3), Yokosuka, Japan (3), Pascagoula, Mississippi (3), and Norfolk, Virginia (7).

Length: 567 feet

Displacement: 9,600 tons (full load)

Speed: 30+ knots

Crew: 24 officers; 340 other ranks

Armament: Mk. 26 launcher (CG 47–51) or Mk. 41 vertical launching system (CG 52–73) for the Standard missile (MR); vertical launch ASROC (VLA) AS missiles; Tomahawk cruise missiles; six Mk. 46 torpedoes in two triple mounts; two Mk. 45 five-inch guns; two Phalanx CIWSs

Aircraft: Two SH-2 Seasprite (LAMPS) helicopters (CG 47–48); two SH-60 Sea Hawk (LAMPS III) on CG 49–73

BELOW: The AEGIS guided-missile cruiser USS *Cape St. George* (CG 71) launches a BGM-109 Tomahawk cruise missile from its aft vertical launcher during Operation Iraqi Freedom.
U.S. Navy photo by Intelligence Specialist 1st Class Kenneth Moll

RIGHT: USS *Vincennes* (CG 49) conducts a high-speed run in the Sea of Japan.
U.S. Navy photo by Photographer's Mate 2nd Class Dennis Cantrell

RIGHT: USS *Philippine Sea* (CG 58) cruises alongside USS *Arctic* (AOE 8) to take on fuel and water during an RAS while en route to the Mediterranean as part of a scheduled six-month deployment.
U.S. Navy photo by Photographer's Mate 1st Class Martin Maddock

BELOW RIGHT: USS *Antietam* (CG 54) breaks away from the aircraft carrier USS *Carl Vinson* (CVN 70) after a refueling at sea.
U.S. Navy photo by Photographer's Mate Third Class Martin S. Fuentes

FAR RIGHT: Waves crash over the bow of USS *Princeton* (CG 59) while receiving nearly 100,000 gallons of JP-5 jet fuel from the aircraft carrier USS *Nimitz* (CVN 68) during an underway replenishment off the California coast.
U.S. Navy photo by Airman Apprentice Mark Rebilas

FOLLOWING PAGES (86/87):
PAGE 86: The guided-missile cruiser USS *Gettysburg* (CG 64) approaches MSC oiler *Tippacanoe* (T-AO 199) as the aircraft carrier USS *Enterprise* (CVN 65) makes ready for another RAS.
U.S. Navy photo by Photographer's Mate 2nd Class Michael W. Pendergrass

PAGE 87: Sailors aboard USS *Anzio* (CG 68) man the rails and search for their family members and friends on a crowded pier as the ship arrives at its homeport at Norfolk Naval Station in Virginia, following a six-month deployment to the Arabian Gulf in support of Operation Iraqi Freedom.
U.S. Navy photo by Photographer's Mate 3rd Class Sondra Howett

RIGHT: The guided-missile cruiser USS *Normandy* (CG 60) comes alongside USS *George Washington* (CVN 73) to conduct an RAS in the Atlantic Ocean.
U.S. Navy photo by Photographer's Mate 3rd Class Lisa Marcus

FAR RIGHT: This five-inch 54-caliber lightweight Mk. 45 gun mount, one of two carried by the AEGIS guided-missile cruiser USS *San Jacinto* (CG 56), provides accurate naval gunfire against fast, highly maneuverable surface and shore targets, along with air threats.
U.S. Navy photo by Photographer's Mate 1st Class Michael W. Pendergrass

BELOW: A signalman aboard the USS *Carl Vinson* (CVN 70) communicates with the guided-missile cruiser USS *Princeton* (CG 59) using a signal lamp.
U.S. Navy photo by Photographer's Mate Airman Inez Lawson

ABOVE: A Finish Rauma-class fast patrol boat, passes down the starboard side of the AEGIS guided-missile cruiser USS *Vella Gulf* (CG 72) in the Baltic Sea during the annual maritime exercise Baltic Operations 2003, run in concert with 12 regional nations.
U.S. Navy photo by Photographer's Mate 2nd Class Michael Sandberg

RIGHT: After pulling away from the pier at Naval Station 32nd Street in San Diego, California, the AEGIS guided-missile cruiser USS *Valley Forge* (CG 50), heads out to begin a scheduled six-month deployment to the western Pacific.
U.S. Navy photo by Photographer's Mate 1st Class Chuck Cavanaugh

ABOVE: The U.S. Navy's AEGIS guided-missile cruiser USS *Chosin* (CG 65) enforces an exclusionary perimeter as the commercial oil tanker *Ab Qaiq* readies itself to receive oil at the Mina-Al-Bkar oil terminal as the first commercial vessel to receive exported Iraqi oil as an offshore customer since 1991.
U.S. Navy photo by Photographer's Mate 2nd Class Andrew M. Meyers

RIGHT: USS *Cape St. George* (CG 71) launches a BGM-109 Tomahawk land-attack cruise missile from its forward vertical launcher against a target in Iraqi during Operation Iraqi Freedom from the eastern Mediterranean Sea.
U.S. Navy photo by Intelligence Specialist 1st Class Kenneth Moll

FAR RIGHT: USS *Shiloh* (CG 67) departs the Naval Weapons Station at Seal Beach, California after offloading weapons and munitions, following its return from a deployment in support of Operation Iraqi Freedom.
U.S. Navy photo by Journalist 2nd Class Brian Brannon

FAR LEFT: USS *Princeton* (CG 59) cuts through the water while deployed in support of Operation Iraqi Freedom in 2003.
U.S. Navy photo by Photographer's Mate 2nd Class Michael J. Pusnik, Jr.

LEFT: Sailors launch a "killer tomato" target prior to running a small-arms training exercise aboard the cruiser USS *Vella Gulf* (CG 72) during the annual Baltic Operations maritime exercise.
U.S. Navy photo by Photographer's Mate 2nd Class Michael Sandberg

RIGHT: The Executive Officer of the aircraft carrier USS *Carl Vinson* (CVN 70), Commander Mike Manazir, is sent across to the guided-missile cruiser USS *Antietam* (CG 54) on a synthetic highline personnel transfer rig.
U.S. Navy photo by Photographer's Mate 3rd Class Kerryl Cacho

BELOW: The guided-missile cruiser USS *Chosin* (CG 65) steams away after completing an underway RAS with the fast combat support ship USS *Bridge* (AOE 10) while deployed in support of Operation Iraqi Freedom with the aircraft carrier USS *Nimitz* (CVN 68).
U.S. Navy photo by Photographer's Mate 3rd Class Yesenia Rosas

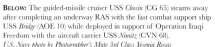

RIGHT: At sea aboard USS *Hue City* (CG 66)—a CH-46 helicopter from the Helicopter Combat Support Squadron HC-6 prepares to pick up a pallet of supplies from *Hue City*. HC-6 was deployed aboard the fast combat support ship USS *Seattle* (AOE 3) during Operation Enduring Freedom.
U.S. Navy photo by Chief Photographer's Mate Spike Call

ABOVE: A cloud of propellant-gas discharge is expelled from the forward five-inch Mk. 45 gun mount aboard the AEGIS cruiser USS *Vella Gulf* (CG 72) during the annual maritime exercise Baltic Operations 2003.
U.S. Navy photo by Photographer's Mate 2nd Class Michael Sandberg

LEFT: Line handlers stand at the ready as USS *Anzio* (CG 68) approaches the pier at its homeport at the Norfolk Naval Base in Virginia following a six-month deployment to the Arabian Gulf in support of Operation Iraqi Freedom.
U.S. Navy photo by Photographer's Mate 3rd Class Sondra Howett

FAR LEFT: USS *Philippine Sea* (CG 58) conducts work-ups prior to its upcoming six-month deployment.
U.S. Navy photo by Photographer's Mate 2nd Class Aaron Peterson

ABOVE: An F/A-18 Hornet fighter-bomber belonging to the U.S. Navy's elite Blue Angels flight demonstration team performs a fly-by of the guided-missile cruiser USS *Thomas S. Gates* (CG 51) in the Gulf of Mexico.
U.S. Navy photo by Gary Nichols

LEFT: Crewmembers assist in the inflight refueling of an SH-60 Seahawk from the flight-deck of USS *Vincennes* (CG 49).
U.S. Navy photo by Photographer's Mate 2nd Class Dennis Cantrell

ABOVE: Crewmembers assigned to the Ticonderoga-class cruiser USS *Vella Gulf* (CG 72) conduct a small-arms exercise. U.S. naval vessels regularly conduct such training, to protect against attacks by swimmers, boats, and small aircraft.
U.S. Navy photo by Photographer's Mate 2nd Class Michael Sandberg

LEFT: USS *Lake Champlain* (CG 57) comes alongside the aircraft carrier USS *John C. Stennis* (CVN 74) for fuel replenishment.
U.S. Navy photo by Photographer's Mate 3rd Class William K. Fletcher

RIGHT: An SH-60B Seahawk assigned to Helicopter Anti-submarine Squadron HS-15—the "Red Lions"—departs USS *Normandy* for its return flight to the aircraft carrier USS *George Washington* (CVN 73) while supporting Operation Enduring Freedom.
U.S. Navy photo by Photographer's Mate 3rd Class T.J. Talarico

BELOW: An EA-6B Prowler from the "Patriots"—Tactical Electronic Warfare Squadron VAQ-140—is prepared for launching from the number four catapult on the angled flightdeck of USS *John F. Kennedy* as the guided-missile cruiser USS *Hue City* (CG 66) passes down the aircraft carrier's port side.

U.S. Navy photo by Photographer's Mate Airman Sherry Hubbard

RIGHT: The AEGIS guided-missile cruiser USS *Vincennes* (CG 49) conducts a crash stop maneuver in the Sea of Japan during training exercises.

U.S. Navy photo by Photographer's Mate 2nd Class Dennis Cantrell

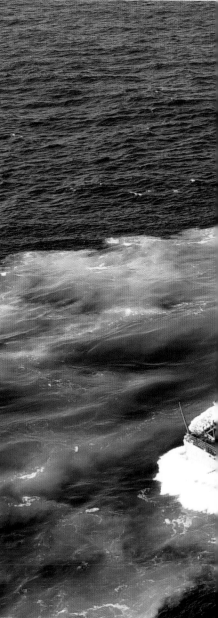

RIGHT: The AEGIS guided-missile cruiser USS *Philippine Sea* (CG 58) departs from its homeport of Mayport, Florida, for a week-long work-up period before an upcoming six-month deployment.
U.S. Navy photo by Photographer's Mate 2nd Class Aaron Peterson

ABOVE): USS *San Jacinto* (CG 56) glides through the Atlantic Ocean off the coast of Florida during a Joint Task Force Exercise prior to a six-month overseas deployment. The two weapons in the foreground are .50-caliber machine guns.
U.S. Navy photo by Photographer's Mate 1st Class Michael W. Pendergrass

FAR RIGHT: As seen from the fantail of the USS *Blue Ridge* (LCC-19) are the Ticonderoga-class cruiser USS *Vincennes* (CG 49—right) and the Arleigh Burke-class destroyer USS *John S. McCain* (DDG 56—left). They were involved in Y2K readiness-testing maneuvers.
U.S. Navy photo by Photographer's Mate 1st Class Wade McKinnon

LEFT: The crew of USS *Shiloh* (CG 67) mans the rails as she passes under the Golden Gate Bridge on her way to San Francisco for the parade of ships during fleet week.
U.S. Navy photo by Journalist 2nd Class M. Shewman

RIGHT: AEGIS cruiser USS *Valley Forge* (CG 50) follows the guided-missile destroyer USS *Preble* (DDG 88) as it fires an SM-2 surface-to-air Standard Missile during exercises off the southern California coast.
U.S. Navy photo by Photographer's Mate 2nd Class Juan Eduardo Diaz

FAR RIGHT: Sailors aboard the USS *Vella Gulf* (CG 72) heave on a stanchion line to receive a fuel line during the underway replenishment with the German oiler FGS *Rhoen* (A 1443) during the Baltic Operations 2003 maritime exercise.
U.S. Navy photo by Photographer's Mate 2nd Class Michael Sandberg

ABOVE: The guided-missile cruiser USS *Antietam* (CG 54) underway
in the rough seas of the East China Sea while on a six-month
deployment.
U.S. Navy photo by Photographer's Mate Airman Aaron Hampton

RIGHT: A Puma helicopter replenishes ships in the USS *Theodore
Roosevelt* (CVN 71) Battle Group.
U.S. Navy photo by Chief Photographer's Mate Eric A. Clement

FAR RIGHT: USS *Hue City* (CG 66) steams alongside the fast combat
support ship USS *Seattle* (AOE 3) during an underway replenishment
at sea while deployed in support of Operation Enduring Freedom.
U.S. Navy photo by Chief Photographer's Mate Spike Call

Destroyers

The U.S. Navy currently deploys two types of destroyers—the ships of the Arleigh Burke class, which are designated guided-missile destroyers (DDG) and those of the Spruance type, which are classified general destroyers (DD). Although the former is the more modern and combat flexible, both are fast warships fitted with offensive and defensive weapons systems so that they can function independently or as an integral part of carrier battle groups, surface warfare forces, amphibious task groups, or at-sea replenishment units. The surviving DDs are primarily equipped for anti-submarine tasks while the DDGs can perform not only this role but also anti-air and anti-surface warfare role. Many of the Spruances have also been retrospectively fitted with the Tomahawk cruise missile system to perform the long-range offensive operations that the DDGs already undertake.

PREVIOUS PAGES (112/113):
The guided-missile destroyer
USS *Cole* (DDG 67) arrives at
pier 4 at Ingalls Shipyard in
preparation for an extensive
repair period after the terrorist
attack in Aden, Yemen left a 40
foot by 40 foot gaping hole in
her port side.
*U.S. Navy photo by Chief
Photographer's Mate Johnny R.
Wilson*

RIGHT: Quartermaster Seaman
Apprentice Matthew Bjorge
plots the ship's course on the
bridge aboard the destroyer
USS *Deyo* (DD 989). *Deyo* was
operating in support of the USS
Harry S. Truman (CVN 75)
CVBG conducting a joint task
force exercise.
*U.S. Navy photo by Photographer's
Mate 1st Class Tina M. Ackerman*

CENTER RIGHT: The guided-
missile destroyer USS *John S.
McCain* (DDG 56) steams in
formation with USS *Kitty Hawk*
(CV 63) and vessels attached to
the Japanese Maritime Self-
Defense Force (JMSDF) and the
U.S. Navy.
*U.S. Navy photo by Photographer's
Mate 3rd Class John Sullivan*

FAR RIGHT: Underway in the
Atlantic Ocean, the guided
missile destroyer USS *Gonzalez*
(DDG 66) conducts work-ups
before an upcoming six-month
deployment. *Gonzalez* is part of
the *Enterprise* Carrier Strike
Group.
*U.S. Navy photo by Photographer's
Mate 2nd Class Aaron Peterson*

Arleigh Burke Class

The first ship of the class, the *Arleigh Burke* (DDG 51),
was launched on July 4, 1991, heralding a construction
program at the facilities run by the Bath Iron Works and
Ingalls Shipbuilding aimed at replacing the destroyers of
the outdated Charles F. Adams and Farragut classes.
Named after a renowned commander of a World War II
destroyer squadron and subsequent chief of naval
operations, the new class marked a quantum leap in U.S.
destroyer design that made the vessels among the most
powerful surface warships in service. Incorporating
an all-steel superstructure and a propulsion system
comprising four General Electric LM 2500–30 gas
turbines powering two shafts, the DDGs also deploy
the AEGIS combat system and the Lockheed Martin
SP-1 radar and combat integrator system to track and
prioritize multiple threats that can be neutralized by
their anti-air, anti-surface, and anti-submarine warfare
systems. The class, which has a combat range of around
4,400 miles at 20 knots, has also been given a long-range
offensive action system by the addition of vertically
launched Tomahawk cruise missiles at two positions—
one between the forward gun mounting and bridge and
the other just forward of the rear flightdeck. At present,
the 40 active DDGs are based at San Diego, California
(12), Mayport, Florida (3), Pearl Harbor, Hawaii (5),
Yokosuka, Japan (2), Norfolk, Virginia (17), and Everett,
Washington (1). Aside from these, one is under
construction, the USS *Pinckney* (DDG 91), and a further
eight (DDG 92–99) are planned.

Length: 504.5 feet (DDG 51–78); 509.5 feet (DDG 79 on)
Displacement (full load): 8,315 tons (DDG 51–71);
   8,400 tons (DDG 72–78); 9,200 tons (DDG 79 on)
Speed: 30+ knots
Crew: 23 officers; 300 other ranks
Armament: Standard SAMs, eight Harpoon SAMs
   mounted on two quad launchers; vertically-launched
   ASROC (VLA) AS missiles, Tomahawk cruise
   missiles; six Mk. 46 torpedoes in two triple mounts;
   one Mk. 45 five-inch gun; two Phalanx CIWSs
Aircraft: Two SH-60 Sea Hawk (LAMPS III) helicopters

ABOVE: The destroyer USS *Nicholson* (DD 982) cruises by Norfolk Waterside as it makes its way to Chesapeake Bay en route to Wilmington, Delaware. Like many older U.S. Navy ships, *Nicholson* has been updated with new systems such as the RAM SAM system launcher on the fantail.
U.S. Navy photo by Photographer's Mate 1st Class Johnny Bivera

RIGHT: The AEGIS guided-missile destroyer *Choukai* (DDG 176) of the Japanese Maritime Self-Defense Force breaks away from formation alongside USS *Kitty Hawk* (CV 63). Based on the American Arleigh Burke-class destroyers, *Choukai* is one of the most capable warships in the service of the Japanese Maritime Self-Defense Force.
U.S. Navy photo by Photographer's Mate Airman Apprentice Michael D. Winter

FAR RIGHT: HMAS *Brisbane* (DDG 41) and USS *John S. McCain* (DDG 56) cruise side by side in Australian waters supporting operations during Exercise Tandem Thrust 2001, a combined U.S. and Australian military training exercise held in the Shoalwater Bay Training Area off the coast of Australia.
U.S. Navy photo by Andrew Meyers

ABOVE: The Spruance-class destroyer USS *Thorn* (DD 988) steams off the starboard quarter of USS *Enterprise* (CVN 65) during its final preparation for the *Enterprise* Strike Group deployment to the Mediterranean.
U.S. Navy photo by Photographer's Mate Airman Joshua Helgeson

LEFT: A line of destroyers, including USS *Thorn* (at right), USS *Cole* (DDG 67), and USS *Gonzalez* (DDG 66, at left), perform divisional tactics while underway in the Atlantic Ocean.
U.S. Navy photo by Photographer's Mate 2nd Class Aaron Peterson

FAR LEFT: The guided-missile destroyer USS *Cole* (DDG 67), despite having been severely damaged by an Al Qaida suicide boat bombing in 2002, steams repaired and ready through the Atlantic Ocean during final preparation for deployment to the Mediterranean.
U.S. Navy photo by Photographer's Mate 2nd Class Douglas M. Pearlman

LEFT: Fireworks and holiday lights liven up the evening sky as the guided-missile frigate USS *Vandergrift* (FFG 48) and destroyer USS *John S. McCain* (DDG 56) bring in the New Year while docked in Yokosuka, Japan.

U.S. Navy photo by Photographer's Mate 3rd Class Lamel J. Hinton

Above: The AEGIS guided-missile destroyer USS *Gonzalez* (DDG 66) is silhouetted as it pulls alongside USS *Enterprise* (CVN 65) for an RAS during Atlantic Fleet carrier qualifications.

U.S. Navy photo by Photographer's Mate 2nd Class Marlow Dix

ABOVE: The U.S. Navy AEGIS cruiser, USS *Lake Erie* (CG 70), conducting the AEGIS Intercept Flight Test Round (FTR-1A) mission at the Pacific Missile range headquartered in the mid-Pacific on the island of Kauai, Hawaii, firing an SM-3 Standard Missile.
U.S. Navy photo

RIGHT: An Arleigh Burke-class destroyer fires a vertically launched SM-2 Standard surface-to-air missile during fleet operations in the Pacific.
U.S. Navy photo

LEFT: A new-model Tactical Tomahawk cruise missile launches from the guided missile destroyer *USS Stethem* (DDG 63) during a live-warhead test, before it traveled 760 nautical miles to successfully impact its intended target on San Clemente Island, part of the Naval Air Systems Command (NAVAIR) test range in Southern California.
U.S. Navy photo

OPPOSITE PAGE, LEFT: The guided-missile destroyer *O'Kane* (DDG 77) fires a SM-2 Standard surface-to-air missile as part of the ship's final sea trials prior to commissioning in August 1999.
U.S. Navy photo by Photographer's Mate 3rd Class Phil Hartman

OPPOSITE PAGE, RIGHT: A Standard SM-2 Block IVA surface to air missile, is fired from the guided-missile destroyer USS *Higgins* (DDG 76) during a live missile fire exercise. Live fire operations gives the ship's crew the experience of launching operational weapons and helps hone their war-fighting skills.
U.S. Navy photo by Photographer's Mate Airman Apprentice Rebecca J. Moat

PREVIOUS PAGES (124/125):

PAGE 124, LEFT: The guided-missile destroyer USS *Cole* (DDG 67), repaired following a terrorist suicide bombing in Yemen in 2000, steams through the Atlantic Ocean during final preparation for deployment to the Mediterranean.
U.S. Navy photo by Photographer's Mate 2nd Class Douglas M. Pearlman

PAGE 124, RIGHT: Electronics Technician 1st Class Mark Caprio checks radar equipment high above the deck of the AEGIS guided-missile destroyer USS *Carney* (DDG 64) while deployed to the Persian Gulf.
U.S. Navy photo by Photographer's Mate 2nd Class Photo Felix Garza

PAGE 125: Silhouetted by the sun and clouds, USS *Carney* patrols the waters of the Persian Gulf.
U.S. Navy photo by Photographer's Mate 2nd Class Photo Felix Garza

RIGHT: The guided-missile destroyer USS *Cole* (DDG 67), repaired following a terrorist suicide bombing in Yemen in 2000, steams through the Atlantic Ocean during final preparation for deployment to the Mediterranean.
U.S. Navy photo by Photographer's Mate 2nd Class Douglas M. Pearlman

FAR RIGHT: Sailors man the rails of USS *Mustin* (DDG 89) and a new warship is brought to life by her crew during a twilight commissioning ceremony held at North Island Naval Air Station. *Mustin* is the 39th Arleigh Burke-class (DDG 51) guided-missile destroyer and is named in honor of four members of a distinguished Navy family with a legacy of naval service stretching over a century. *U.S. Navy photo by Photographer's Mate 3rd Class John DeCoursey*

ABOVE: The Aegis guided-missile destroyer USS *Donald Cook* (DDG 75) cruises past the starboard-side hangar bay of the USS *George Washington* (CVN 73) in the Arabian Gulf.
U.S. Navy photo by Ensign Philip St. Gelais

RIGHT: During a simulated small craft attack, the guided missile destroyer USS *Benfold* (DDG 65) takes aim at the enemy "mother ship" with her forward Mk. 45 5-inch dual purpose gun.
U.S. Navy Photo by Photographer's Mate 2nd Class Michael D. Kennedy.

RIGHT: The Arkeigh Burke-class guided-missile destroyer USS *Higgins* (DDG 76) sails under a drawbridge on the Willamette River during arrival ceremonies for the annual Rose Festival in Portland, Oregon.
U.S. Navy photo by Photographer's Mate 2nd Class Mike Larson

FAR RIGHT: The AEGIS guided-missile destroyer USS *Winston S. Churchill* (DDG 81) makes a high-speed run in the English Channel. The ship is named in honor of Sir Winston Spencer Leonard Churchill (1874-1965), best known for his courageous leadership as British Prime Minister of Great Britian during World War II.
U.S. Navy photo by Photographer's Mate 2nd Class Shane T. McCoy

Spruance Class

At present, the Spruance-class DDs are undergoing a major modernization program after first entering service on September 20, 1975, the day the *Spruance* itself was launched. Originally constructed to replace the Gearing and Allen M. Summer classes that had first appeared during World War II, the new destroyers, all of which have been built by Ingall Shipbuilding of Pascagoula, Mississippi, had more that twice the displacement of the older designs. The aim was to create a roomy vessel that eased maintenance and also allowed for the subsequent fitting of updated electronics and weapons systems, thereby giving them a greater life expectancy. The new destroyers were also the first large ships in the U.S. Navy to use gas-turbine engines and are currently fitted with four General Electric LM 2500–30s that generate 80,000 total shaft horsepower. The value of the large design has proved invaluable in an ongoing update program on 24 of the class. This includes the addition of a more advanced anti-submarine warfare combat system, a larger helicopter capability, and the provision of Tomahawk cruise missiles that can be vertically launched or fired from armored box launchers. Although close to 30 years old the Spruances are expected to see service well into the present century. At the time of writing the nine of the modernized Spruance class are back in service and are based at San Diego, California (1), Mayport Florida (2), Pearl Harbor, Hawaii (1), Yokosuka, Japan (2), and Norfolk, Virginia (3).

Length: 563 feet

Displacement: 8,040 tons (full load)

Speed: 30+ knots

Crew: 30 officers; 352 other ranks

Armament: Generally eight Harpoon SAMs; vertically launched ASROC AS missiles; vertically or armored box-launched Tomahawk cruise missiles; six Mk. 46 torpedoes in two triple mounts; two Mk. 45 five-inch guns; two Phalanx CIWSs. (Note: Four carried NATO's Sea Sparrow point defense anti-air missiles. These modified Spruances were renamed the Kidd class (DDG 993–996) and originally intended for Iran but were retained by the U.S. Navy following the overthrown of the Shah of Iran in 1979)

Aircraft: Two SH-60 Sea Hawk (LAMPS III) helicopters

RIGHT: The destroyer USS *Arthur W. Radford* (DD 968) undergoing extensive repairs at Norfolk Naval Shipyard in Portsmouth, Virginia, following a collision at sea with a foreign vessel in February 1999. The Portsmouth yard workers replaced the ship's bow and five-inch Mk. 45 gun mount, closed a 21-foot hole in her side, and did other major work in just three months.
U.S. Navy photo courtesy of Mel Gipson

FAR RIGHT: The destroyer USS *Fletcher* (DD 992) navigates alongside USNS *Pecos* (T-AU197) in preparation for an RAS in the North Arabian Gulf.
U.S. Navy photo by Photographer's Mate 2nd Class Christopher Mobley

RIGHT: The destroyer USS *Thorn* (DD 988) speeds through the waters of the Atlantic Ocean to come alongside USS *Enterprise* (CVN 65) to conduct a VERTREP.
U.S. Navy photo by Photographer's Mate Airman Frank Jakubec

FAR RIGHT: USS *Elliott* (DD 967) is guided into pier 7 at Naval Station 32nd Street, San Diego, California, by a tugboat after a six-month deployment to the Western Pacific and Indian Ocean.
U.S. Navy photo by Photographer's Mate 1st Class Chuck Cavanaugh

RIGHT: An aerial view of the destroyer USS *Fletcher* (DD 992) operating in the Arabian Gulf in support of Exercise Arabian Shark 2000. The destroyer is lowering a rubber boat in preparation for simulating a maritime boarding and examination.
U.S. Navy photo by Photographer's Mate 1st Class David J. Weideman

CENTER RIGHT: USS *Nicholson* (DD 982) cruises by tall ships involved in OpSail 2000, a celebration of maritime tradition and the cooperation of over sixty nations.
U.S. Navy photo by Photographer's Mate 1st Class Johnny Bivera

FAR RIGHT: Crewmembers aboard the destroyer USS *Deyo* (DD 989) transfer packaged powder charges to the five-inch Mk. 45 gun mount while operating in the Atlantic during a joint task force exercise.
U.S. Navy photo by Photographer's Mate 1st Class Tina M. Ackerman

RIGHT: The Spruance-class destroyer USS *Cushing* (DD 985) steams toward a merchant vessel suspected of carrying contraband cargo in the Arabian Gulf prior to Operation Iraqi Freedom.
U.S. Navy photo by Photographer's Mate 2nd Class Michael Sandberg

FAR RIGHT: USS *Arthur W. Radford* (DD 968) arrives for a brief port visit at Suda Bay, Crete. This Spruance-class destroyer has been used as a testbed for a new composite mast, which is being used to evaluate various options for construction of more stealthy future warship designs.
U.S. Navy photo by Paul Farley

FOLLOWING PAGES (138/139):
PAGE 138: Signalman 2nd Class Patrick Fisher stands atop the capstan of a tugboat and prepares to throw a line as it pulls alongside the destroyer USS *Stump* (DD 978) at Norfolk Naval Station in Norfolk, Virginia.
U.S. Navy photo by Photographer's Mate Airman Apprentice Saul Ingle

PAGE 139: The destroyer USS *Briscoe* (DD 977) makes its approach for an RAS with the USS *George Washington* (CVN 73) off the Virginia Capes.
U.S. Navy photo by Photographer's Mate 3rd Class Corey Lewis

Frigates

The Oliver Hazard Perry-class warships are the only frigates remaining in service with the U.S. Navy and there are no plans to develop any further such vessels. The *Oliver Hazard Perry* (no longer in service) was launched on December 17, 1977, and today 30 of its sisters remain on the active list. They are designated guided missile frigates (FFG) and are primarily deployed to protect other surface vessels, particularly amphibious assault groups, at-sea replenishment forces, and merchant convoys. Radar and weapons systems give them both anti-submarine and anti-air capabilities but these frigates lack the true multi-role flexibility of the most modern U.S. warships.

THIS PAGE: An RHIB crew assigned to the U.S. Navy frigate USS *Samuel B. Roberts* (FFG 58) look on as their ship arrives for a scheduled port visit at Suda Bay, Crete, while assigned to NATO's Standing Naval Force Mediterranean.
U.S. Navy photo by Paul Farley

RIGHT: USS *Thach* (FFG 43) shows her holiday lights while tied up at Pier 54, Naval Station 32nd Street in San Diego, California.
U.S. Navy photo by Photographer's Mate 1st Class Charles P. Cavanaugh

Oliver Hazard Perry Class

The original naval requirement, which emerged in the 1970s, was for a frigate that had to be easy to construct by making use of prefabricated modules of 35, 100, 200, or 400 tons, with the intention of building a large number of vessels (more than 40) at relatively low cost. On this basis the U.S. government also laid down strict criteria regarding displacement and crew numbers and also requested that tried and tested radar, weapons, and propulsion systems be used in the design, and that there should be little room left over for adding updated equipment in the future. For example, the frigate's pair of General Electric LM 2500 gas turbine engines are the same as those already fitted to Spruance class destroyers. The envisaged frigate did not have to be particularly fast but did have to have excellent endurance, some 4,500 miles at 20 knots, to carry out its protection and escort roles. Construction of the finalized warship was allocated to three shipyards—the Bath Iron Works and two Todd Shipyards, one in Seattle, Washington, and the other at San Pedro, California—but to ensure that the agreed design was mission-capable the *Oliver Hazard Perry* (FFG 7) was built and then tested for two years to iron out any teething troubles before construction of the remaining warships was initiated. These were mostly completed on time or ahead of schedule and close to the pre-agreed cost. Today, the surviving frigates are based in San Diego, California (5), Mayport, Florida (9), Pearl Harbor, Hawaii (2), Yokosuka, Japan (2), Pascagoula, Mississippi (2), Norfolk, Virginia (7), and Everett, Washington (3).

Length: 445 feet

Displacement: 4,100 tons (full load)

Speed: 29+ knots

Crew: 17 officers; 198 other ranks

Armament: Standard SAMs (MR); Harpoon SSMs fired from Standard missile launcher, six Mk. 46 torpedoes fired from two triple mounts; single Mk. 75 three-inch gun; single Phalanx CIWS

Aircraft: Two SH-60 Sea Hawk (LAMPS III) (FFG 8, 28, 29, 32, 33, 36–61); single SH-2 Seasprite (LAMPS I) (FFG 9–19, 30, 31)

BELOW: The guided missile frigate USS *Reid* (FFG 30) fights through heavy seas at it approaches the supply ship USS *Rainier* (AOE 7), during an underway replenishment operation in the western Pacific.
U.S. Navy photo by Photographer's Mate 3rd Class Weathers

RIGHT: USS *McClusky* (FFG 41) practices evasion maneuvers in the Pacific Ocean as part of a bilateral military force for Exercise RIMPAC 98.
U.S. Navy photo by Photographer's Mate 1st Class Spike Call

BELOW: The guided-missile frigate USS *Kauffman* (FFG 59) arrives for a brief port visit to Suda Bay, Crete while operating on a six-month deployment in support of Operation Enduring Freedom.
U.S. Navy photo by Paul Farley

LEFT: A sailor stands watch as aft lookout on the fantail of the guided missile frigate USS *Vandegrift* (FFG 48) in heavy seas while operating off the coast of Japan.
U.S. Navy photo by Chief Aviation Structural Mechanic Douglas Waddell

RIGHT: USS *Thach* (FFG 43) gets underway while on deployment in the South Pacific, en route to the port of Sydney, Australia.
U.S. Navy photo by Photographer's Mate 1st Class Anthony C. Casullo

LEFT: The guided missile frigate USS *Klakring* (FFG 42) navigates the tight canyons and fjords of the Inter-Chilean Waterway during a transit from Valparaiso, Chile, to Argentina around the southern tip of South America during UNITAS 2000, the annual international exercise held by the navies of Latin America.
U.S. Navy photo by Lt (JG) Corey Barker

FAR LEFT: Torpedoman 3rd Class David Saldana fires an air slug from a Mk. 32 lightweight torpedo launcher aboard the guided missile frigate USS *Reuben James* (FFG 57) in support of the Cooperation Afloat Readiness and Training 2000 exercise.
U.S. Navy photo by Photographer's Mate 1st Class Spike Call

Submarines

The U.S. Navy has three types of submarine at its disposal. All are nuclear-powered and are designated SSBN (submarine, ballistic missile, nuclear), SSN (submarine, attack, nuclear), or SSGN (submarine, guided missile, nuclear). Each is tasked with a different function, from the strategic to tactical, although the SSNs and SSGNs are equipped with similar weaponry. The SSBNs of the Ohio class primarily carry the Trident long-range multi-warhead nuclear missiles that are the cornerstone of the United States' strategic defense forces. The SSN force comprises three classes— Virginia, Sea Wolf, and Los Angeles—and are armed to attack enemy submarines and surface ships or hit land-based targets. The SSGNs are modified Ohio-class submarines configured to launch tactical long-range missiles as well as deploy special operations forces for clandestine missions.

THIS PAGE: The nuclear powered ballistic submarine, USS *Rhode Island* (SSBN 740) leaves for an Atlantic deterrence patrol mission from Kings Bay, Georgia. *U.S. Navy photo by Patrick Nugent*

Ohio Class

This class of large submarines is the sea-based arm of the U.S. nuclear deterrence force and was introduced into service with the launching of the name ship of the class, the USS *Ohio* (SSBN 726), on November 11, 1981. Each of the 18 original Ohio submarines was fitted to carry multi-warhead Trident ballistic missiles; the first eight carried the C-4 version and all now carry the highly accurate Trident II D-5, which was first introduced on the ninth vessel in the class, the USS *Tennessee* (SSBN 734). The Ohios were built to replace the ageing ballistic missile submarines that entered service during the 1960s and their ongoing importance in the nation's strategic defense forces can be estimated by the fact that they carry around 50 percent of the total strategic nuclear warheads available at the present. Details concerning their patrols are obviously classified but it is known that they can stay at sea and submerged for long periods and that, while their missiles are not pretargeted, rapid and secure communications ensure that they can be deployed at short notice. The original four Ohio-class submarines (SSBN 726–729) are being converted to SSGNs and on October 29, 2002, the *Ohio* was the first of these taken out of service for the necessary upgrade to carry Tomahawk cruise missiles and special forces. The 14 submarines that will continue in the deterrence role comprise the six based at Bangor, Washington (SSBN 730–737), and the eight at Kings Bay, Georgia (SSBN 734–743).

Data: SSBN (Trident)
Length: 560 feet
Displacement: 16,764 tons (surface); 18,750 tons (submerged)
Speed: 20+ knots
Crew: 15 officers; 140 other ranks
Armament: Twenty-four tubes for Trident Mks. I or II long-range, multiple warhead nuclear ballistic missiles; four 21-inch bow tubes for Mk. 48 torpedoes

Continued on page 154.

ABOVE: An artist's concept of USS *Ohio* (SSGN 726), which is undergoing a conversion from a ballistic missile submarine to a guided missile/special operations configuration. Four Ohio-class strategic missile submarines, USS *Ohio* (SSBN 726), USS *Michigan* (SSBN 727), USS *Florida* (SSBN 728), and USS *Georgia* (SSBN 729) have been selected to have the capability to support and launch up to 154 Tomahawk missiles, along with the capability to carry other payloads, such as unmanned underwater vehicles, unmanned aerial vehicles, or more than 66 Special Operations Personnel, such as U.S. Navy SEALs.
U.S. Navy photo

RIGHT: USS *Ohio* (SSGN 726) in dry dock undergoing conversion to its new configuration. *U.S. Navy photo*

PREVIOUS PAGES (152/153):
PAGE 152: The Ohio-class fleet ballistic missile submarine USS *Henry M. Jackson* (SSBN 730) prepares to get underway.
U.S. Navy photo

PAGE 153: USS *Rhode Island* (SSBN 740) cruises through the Atlantic Ocean as crewmembers work up on deck.
U.S. Navy photo by Journalist 3rd Class B.L. Keller

LEFT: USS *Alabama* (SSBN 731) cruises on the surface as it approaches the Naval Submarine Base at San Diego following the completion of its 50th deterrent patrol.
U.S. Navy photo by Photographer's Mate 1st Class Mark A. Correa

RIGHT: USS *Maine* (SSBN 741), one of the newest Ohio-class submarines, conducts surface operations in heavy seas south of Naval Station Roosevelt Roads, Puerto Rico.
U.S. Navy photo by Photographer's Mate First Class Michael J. Rinaldi

It was initially intended that the first four Ohio-class SSBNs, the USSs *Ohio, Michigan, Florida,* and *Georgia* (SSBN 727–729), were to be withdrawn from service during the financial year 2003–2004 but the decision was taken to convert them to guided missile submarines—SSGNs—with a completion date earmarked for 2008 after a five-year refit program by the General Dynamics Electric Boat Division. When the overhaul is completed each SSGN will be dedicated to land attack missions or the transport and support of special operations forces on clandestine missions. In the former case each will be able to carry 154 Tomahawk or Tactical Tomahawk long-range cruise missiles, while in the latter role they will accommodate up to 60 troops for around 90 days—a vast improvement on the 15 days that was possible for the first batch of modified SSN submarines that had the same capability. To enhance their special forces role the SSGNs are also to be fitted with dual dry deck shelters and/or the Advanced SEAL Delivery System. Aside from these primary missions, the submarines are also able to carry out the more traditional roles associated with such attack craft, including intelligence-gathering, long-range reconnaissance and surveillance of enemy vessels, and attack missions. The *Ohio* went out of service for conversion on October 29, 2002, and the work was undertaken at Puget sound Naval Dockyard; the *Florida* and *Michigan* were scheduled to begin such work in late 2003 and the update of the *Georgia* is penciled in for 2004.

Data: SSGNs
Length: 560 feet
Displacement: 16,764 tons (surfaced); 18,750 tons (submerged)
Speed: 20+ knots
Crew: 15 officers; 140 other ranks
Armament: Up to 154 Tomahawk or Tactical Tomahawk cruise missiles or up to 66 special forces (in which case the number of Tomahawks is reduced to 140)

PREVIOUS PAGES (158/159):
PAGE 158: Tugboats assist the
USS *Pennsylvania* (SSBN 735) as
it arrives at its new homeport at
Bangor, Washington, after
transiting from the navy's east
coast submarine base at Kings
Bay, Georgia.
U.S. Navy photo by Brian Nokell

PAGE 159, LEFT: Crewmembers
aboard USS *Florida* (SSBN 728)
raise the colors prior to getting
underway from Oahu, Hawaii.
*U.S. Navy photo by Photographer's
Mate 3rd Class Diamond*

PAGE 159, RIGHT: USS *Alabama*
(SSBN 731) works alongside the
Explosives Handling Wharf at
the Submarine Base at Bangor,
Washington.
U.S. Navy photo by Brian Nokell

RIGHT: USS *Nebraska* (SSBN
739) underway on the surface
off the Naval Submarine Base
at Kings Bay, Georgia.
*U.S. Navy photo by Photographer's
Mate 3rd Class Christian Viera*

FAR RIGHT: A view looking aft
from the fairweather (sail) of
the nuclear-powered ballistic
submarine USS *Pennsylvania*
(SSBN 735) as the ship cruises
off the coast of Georgia.
U.S. Navy photo by Larry Smith

Los Angeles Class

This class of attack submarines remains the most numerous in service with the U.S. Navy and went into service with the launching of the name ship of the class, the USS *Los Angeles* (SSN 688) on November 13, 1976. All of the class, which are fitted with a single nuclear reactor that powers a single propeller shaft, were built by either the General Dynamics Electric Boat Division or the Newport News Shipbuilding Company. Like other boats of this type in the navy's inventory, their chief role is to attack the enemy's submarines and surface ships in the time-honored tradition with torpedoes fired from their four 21-inch tubes. In addition they carry a variety of Tomahawk cruise missiles for use in the anti-ship role and for neutralizing land targets in association with ground operations. From the USS *Providence* (SSN) onward these were fired by way of a vertical launch system comprising twelve tubes. Harpoon anti-ship missiles and both floating and tethered mines can also be deployed. Four of the class (SSNs 688, 690, 700, and 701) were fitted with dry dock shelters for special operations missions and four others were modified to carry the Advanced Swimmer Delivery System (SSNs 762, 766, 768, and 772). Today there are 51 of these SSNs in service and they are divided between their home bases at San Diego, California (7), Groton, Connecticut (13), Pearl Harbor, Hawaii (16), Guam, Mariana Islands (2), Portsmouth, New Hampshire (1), Norfolk, Virginia (11), and Bremerton, Washington (1).

Length: 360 feet

Displacement: 6,802 tons (surfaced); 6,900 tons (submerged)

Speed: 20+ knots

Crew: 13 officers; 121 other ranks.

Armament: Tomahawk land-attack and surface-to-surface cruise missiles; Harpoon anti-ship missiles; four 21-inch tubes midships for Mk. 48 torpedoes; can also lay both Mk. 67 mobile and Mk. 60 captor mines

ABOVE: Sailors stand topside watch on aboard the fast attack submarine USS *Tucson* (SSN 770) while operating in the Arabian Gulf in support of Exercise Arabian Shark 2000.
U.S. Navy photo by Photographer's Mate 1st Class David J. Weideman

RIGHT: An SH-60F Seahawk from Helicopter Anti-Submarine Squadron HS-5—the "Nightdippers"—deploys its dipping sonar in front of the Sturgeon-class attack submarine, USS *Grayling* (SSN 646) while operating in the western Mediterranean.
U.S. Navy photo by Photographer's Mate 2nd Class Jim Vidrine

RIGHT: USS *Hampton* (SSN 767) crewmembers set a topside watch as they prepare to get underway following a brief port visit to Suda Bay, Crete. Once underway, all of the masts, antennas, rails, and other equipment will be retracted or struck, leaving the sail clear of sound-generating obstructions.
U.S. Navy photo by Paul Farley

RIGHT: Store Keeper Seaman Jeremy Cash looks across the horizon from the bridge aboard the attack submarine USS *Tucson* (SSN 770) as she heads out to sea while participating in Exercise Teamwork South 99 off the coast of Chile.
U.S. Navy photo by Photographer's Mate 1st Class Chris Desmond

CENTER RIGHT: The crew of USS *Tucson* (SSN 770) stand bridge watch as the sub pulls into Tokyo Bay, Japan.
U.S. Navy photo by Photographer's Mate 3rd Class Lamel J. Hinton

FAR RIGHT: The attack submarine USS *Columbus* (SSN 762), based at the Naval Station Pearl Harbor, Hawaii, conducts an "emergency blow" training exercise 35 miles off the coast of Oahu, Hawaii.
U.S. Navy photo by Photographer's Mate 2nd Class David C. Duncan

LEFT: Crew members assigned to the nuclear powered attack submarine USS *Dallas* (SSN 700) make final preparations to get underway for a scheduled overseas deployment.
U.S. Navy photo by Nicole Hawley

BELOW: The nuclear attack submarine USS *Louisville* (SSN 724) returns to Pearl Harbor, Hawaii from a deployment over eight-months duration in support of Operation Iraqi Freedom.
U.S. Navy photo by Photographer's Mate 3rd Class Adan Fabela III

FAR LEFT: The guided-missile cruiser USS *Port Royal* (CG 73) (left) and the submarine USS *Annapolis* (SSN 760) steam in formation with USS *Nimitz* (CVN 68) in the north Persian Gulf in support of Operation Southern Watch.
U.S. Navy photo by Photographer's Mate 2nd Class Matthew J. Magee

LEFT: An aircrewman assigned to Helicopter Anti-Submarine Squadron HS-5—the "Nightdippers"—lowers a package on a rescue hoist from an SH-60F Seahawk to the USS *Boise* (SSN 764) which was operating in support of Operation Enduring Freedom.
U.S. Navy photo by Photographer's Mate 1st Class Jim Hampshire

RIGHT: USS *Tuscon* (SSN 770) cutting though a light sea.
U.S. Navy News Photo

FOLLOWING PAGES (170/171):
PAGE 170: The attack submarine *Seawolf* (SSN 21) conducts her first at-sea trial operations in the Narragansett Bay operating area in the Western Atlantic, following an early morning departure from the Naval Submarine Base, Groton, Connecticut.
U.S. Navy photo Courtesy General Dynamics

PAGE 171, LEFT: Crew members move topside to make final preparations for arrival at Port Canaveral, Florida. *Seawolf* had run submerged for three days during sea trials.
U.S. Navy photo by Chief Photographer John E. Gay

PAGE 171, RIGHT: *Seawolf* heads out to sea to conduct trials in preparation for its commissioning in 1997.
U.S. Navy photo courtesy of Electric Boat Corporation by Jim Brennan

Seawolf Class

With a production cost of around $2.1 billion each and
construction work only beginning in the late 1990s, the
number of submarines in the Seawolf class in service at
the present is small, with just two available at the time of
writing—the USS *Seawolf* (SSN 21) and the USS
Connecticut (SSN 22)—and a further unit undergoing
construction, the USS *Jimmy Carter* (SSN 23). Built by
the General Electric Boat Division, as will be its
immediate sisters, the *Seawolf* itself completed its first sea
trials in 1996 and proved to be fast and well armed for
its missions as well as remarkably quiet when underway.
Like other classes of the U.S. Navy's long-range nuclear
attack submarines, these boats have two main roles: to
find and destroy enemy submarines and surface
warships, and also to support ground operations through
launching SLCMs (submarine-launched cruise missiles),
which were first deployed in anger during Operation
Desert Storm in the early 1990s and proved to be highly
accurate at striking distant targets. To deal with enemy
shipping the Seawolf-class vessels are also armed with
eight 26-inch torpedo tubes and can, if torpedoes are
not carried, deploy up to 100 mines to interdict seaways
and shipping routes. Various sensors, both active and
passive, are fitted to detect targets. Both the *Seawolf* and
Connecticut have their home base at Groton, Connecticut.

Length: 353 feet
Displacement: 8,060 tons (surfaced); 9,150 tons
 (submerged)
Speed: 25+ knots
Crew: 13 officers; 121 other ranks
Armament: Tomahawk land-attack and surface-to-
 surface anti-ship missiles; eight 26-inch tubes for
 Mk. 48 torpedoes; or 100 mines can be carried
 instead of the torpedoes

BELOW: Sailors carefully ready mooring lines aboard USS *Seawolf*
(SSN 21) as she prepares to dock in Port Canaveral, Florida.
U.S. Navy photo by Chief Photographer John E. Gay

RIGHT: USS *Seawolf* heads out into Long Island Sound.
U.S. Navy photo courtesy of Electric Boat Corporation by Jim Brennan

Virginia Class

In the late 1980s and early 1990s, the U.S. Navy began looking at a new type of submarine that could fulfill the multitude of roles as outlined in mission statements entitled "From the Sea" and "Forward ... From the Sea" that reflected the fast-changing geopolitical concerns of the United States following the collapse of the Soviet Union and the ending of the Cold War. A requirement, one based on the need to develop a more flexible submarine force in a more uncertain world, was drawn up for a nuclear-powered, single-shaft submarine that could not only undertake far-flung deep-water missions but could also operate in confined waters and support ground operations. The U.S. Navy wanted to emphasize quality of product over quantity, a well-established request, but also demanded a realistically affordable design. Based on cost estimates revealed in 1995, each of the Virginia-class submarines will cost around $1.65 billion dollars and it is envisaged that the U.S. Navy will receive 30 boats in the years following the go-ahead for the first boat in 1998. At present construction work on four is underway: the USS *Virginia* (SSN 774), which is due for delivery in 2004; the USS *Texas* (SSN 775), which is due in 2005; the USS *Hawaii* (SSN 776) to be ready in 2006, and the USS *North Carolina* (SSN 777) for 2007. The boats are being built at two companies, the General Dynamics Electric Boat Division and Newport News Shipbuilding. At present their home bases have not been revealed and the specifications remain speculative.

Length: 377 feet
Displacement: 7,800 tons (surfaced)
Speed: 25+ knots
Crew: 134 officers and other ranks
Armament: Tomahawk cruise missiles in vertical launch tubes; four tubes for Mk. 48 torpedoes, advanced mobile mines and unmanned undersea vehicles

Amphibious
Warfare Vessels

The U.S. Navy can deploy a number of formidable amphibious warfare groups that incorporate a variety of vessels to transport expeditionary forces around the world and then deploy them ashore by using either conventional or air-cushion landing craft and a range of helicopters. Some also carry helicopter and fixed-wing aircraft to provide immediate fire-support and have anti-submarine warfare capabilities. The range of vessels perform either a single function, such as the AGF and Blue Ridge-class command ships, or can undertake a variety of tasks associated with amphibious forces. Chief among these various types of large vessels are the amphibious assault ships known as LHAs and LHDs and the dock-landing and amphibious transport ships designated LPDs and LSDs. Most of these units are split between the Pacific and Atlantic oceans. Most have their home ports on either the East and West Coast but some are forward-deployed, chiefly at a base in Japan.

LEFT: The U.S. Third Fleet command ship USS *Coronado* (AGF 11) approaches Pier 66 in Seattle, Washington in preperation of mooring in preperation for the opening of Seafair 1999.
U.S. Navy photo by Photographer's Mate 2nd Class Todd R. Cromar

BELOW LEFT: The Command Ship USS *Blue Ridge* (LCC 19) makes a turn in Sydney Harbour on its way to the Naval Dockyard at Wooloomooloo and a well deserved port visit to Sydney, Australia.
U.S. Navy photo by Photographer's Mate 3rd Class Adam Eastman

FAR LEFT: USS *Coronado* (AGF 11), nicknamed "Death Star," steams near Waikiki during Fleet Battle Experiment Bravo.
U.S. Navy photo by Photographer's Mate 2nd Class Ted Banks

FAR LEFT, INSET: A utility landing craft heads for the island of Tinian after leaving the well deck of USS *Fort McHenry* (LSD-43). The LCU was transporting soldiers, marines, and their equipment to the beach in support of Exercise Tandem Thrust '99.
Official U.S. Navy photo

Blue Ridge Class

This class of LCC (landing lraft lommand), which comprises the *Blue Ridge* (LCC 19) and the *Mount Whitney* (LCC 19), was chiefly built to provide command and control facilities for the U.S. Navy's amphibious fleets in the Atlantic and Pacific. They replaced older command vessels dating from World War II that were no longer able to keep up with more modern amphibious warfare ships capable of over 20 knots. Based on the Iwo Jima-class of LPHs (landing platform helicopter), their hangar space was simply converted into command and control rooms, office space, and crew accommodation, while the former flightdeck was modified to take a larger superstructure amidships, a smaller structure aft, and various surveillance, countermeasure, and communications arrays along the line of the deck. The facilities were designed to take the commanders of an amphibious task force, a Marine landing force, and an air control group, along with their staffs. Aside from their crews both vessels were provided with further accommodation that could take around an extra 200 officers and 500 enlisted men. Construction of the class was given to the Philadelphia Naval Shipyard, which built LCC 19, and Newport News Shipbuilding and Docking in Virginia (LCC 20), with the *Blue Ridge* being deployed on November 14, 1970. Although commissioned to undertake the amphibious command role, both ships latterly became fleet flagships. The *Blue Ridge*, which has its home base at Yokosuka, Japan, has filled this role for the U.S. Seventh Fleet since 1979, while the *Mount Whitney* became the U.S. Second Fleet's flagship in 1981 and is based at Norfolk, Virginia.

Length: 634 feet

Displacement: 18,874 tons (full load)

Speed: 23 knots

Crew: 52 officers; 790 other ranks

Armament: Two Phalanx CIWSs

Aircraft: Usually one SH-3H Sea King, although most U.S. Navy helicopters can land with the exception of the CH-53 Sea Stallion

ABOVE: USS *Mount Whitney* (LCC 20) pulls alongside USNS *Patuxent* (AO 201) for an underway replenishment.
U.S. Navy photo by Journalist 2nd Ed Mekeel III

PREVIOUS PAGES (176/177): A utility landing craft (LCU 1630) heads for the island of Tinian after leaving the well deck of USS *Fort McHenry* (LSD-43). The LCU was transporting soldiers, marines, and their equipment to the beach in support of Exercise Tandem Thrust '99.
Official U.S. Navy photo

RIGHT: Sailors man the rails of USS *BonHomme Richard* (LHD 6) as she passes downtown San Diego en route to the Arabian Gulf on her maiden deployment in support of Operation Southern Watch.
U.S. Navy photo by Photographer's Mate 2nd Class David C. Mercil

LEFT: Second Fleet flagship USS *Mount Whitney* (LCC 20) participates in Joint Task Force Exercise 01-3.
U.S. Navy Photo by Photographer's Mate1st Class Joe Bullinger

FAR LEFT: USS *Blue Ridge* (LCC 19) pulls into White Beach, Okinawa, Japan, to disembark sailors and marines temporarily assigned to the ship for training.
U.S. Navy photo by Photographer's Mate Airman Kurt Eischen

LEFT: Amphibious transport ship USS *Trenton* (LPD 14) followed by fleet oiler USS *Merrimack* (AO 179). Both were part of the USS *George Washington* (CVN 73) CVBG in support of NATO-led peacekeeping operations in Bosnia.
U.S. Navy photo by Photographer's Mate 1st Class (Air Warfare) Greg Pinkley

ABOVE: An air-cushion landing craft (LCAC) heads toward the well deck of USS *Denver* (LPD 9) while conducting operations during Exercise Kernel Blitz '97.
U.S. Navy photo by Photographer's Mate Second Class Jeffrey S. Viano

Austin Class

The Austin-class ships are classified as LPD (landing platform deck) and are tasked with transporting and landing on hostile shores assault forces, usually Marines but also small groups of special forces, by helicopter or conventional and air-cushion landing craft. When construction began in the 1960s, twelve units were envisaged and the contracts were parceled out between several shipyards, including New York Naval Shipyard, Ingalls Shipbuilding, and Lockheed Shipbuilding. The named unit of the class, the *Austin* (LPD 4), was deployed on February 6, 1965, and the remainder were completed by 1971, making those still in service in their original role (LPDs 4–10 and 12–15), among the oldest warships in the modern U.S. Navy. The class was designed as a replacement for the two ships of the Raleigh class, the navy's first LPD, that were completed in 1962–63: the main difference was the lengthening of the hull in the Austins by adding a 50-foot section just forward of the aft docking well. This modification dramatically increased the space available below decks for vehicles and cargo by close to 100 percent and permitted the addition of a telescopic hangar for helicopter maintenance immediately behind the superstructure. However, the Austins could accommodate no more troops than the Raleigh class and even less in the case of LPDs 7–13, which were built as amphibious squadron flagships. The eleven Austins remaining are based at San Diego, California (5), Sasebo, Japan (1), and Norfolk, Virginia (5), but they will be decommissioned in stages as the newer San Antonio class enters service.

Length: 570 feet
Displacement: 17,000 tons (full load)
Speed: 21 knots
Crew: 24 officers; 396 other ranks
Armament: Two Mk. 38 25 mm guns; eight 0.5-caliber machine guns; two Phalanx CIWSs
Aircraft: Up to six CH-46 Sea Knight helicopters
Carrying capacity: 900 Marines

San Antonio Class

These vessels, none of which are yet in service, are intended to replace four classes of the U.S. Navy's older amphibious ships. They will make use of stealth technology in the design of their hulls and superstructure, and their primary role will be to transport and deploy various assault forces, from Marine expeditionary units to special forces, by helicopter or landing craft. The contract for building the first in the new class, the *San Antonio* (LPD 17), was agreed in December 1996 and construction began in August 2000 with the work being undertaken by Northrop Grumman Ship Systems aided by Raytheon Systems Corporation, and Intergraph Corporation. By December 2002 more than half of the work on the *San Antonio* had been completed and further units had been contracted to this consortium—the *New Orleans* (LPD 18) in December 1998 and the *Green Bay* (LPD 20) in May 2000. A fourth ship, the *Mesa Verde* (LPD 19), was originally given to the Bath Iron Works in Maine but transferred to Northrop in exchange for the former gaining the contract to build further units of the Arleigh Burke class of guided-missile destroyers. The fifth in the San Antonio class will be named *New York* to commemorate the terrorist attack on the city's Twin Towers on September 11, 2001. Each unit will have some 25,000 square feet of deck space and will also be able to accommodate around 34,000 cubic feet of supplies and cargoes in their holds. In total the U.S. Navy currently has a requirement for twelve San Antonio-class LPDs.

Length: 684 feet
Displacement: 24,900 tons (full load)
Speed: 22+ knots
Crew: 28 officers; 333 other ranks
Armament: Two Rolling Airframe Missile (RAM) launchers; two Bushmaster II CIWSs
Aircraft: Two CH-53E Super Stallion helicopters or up to four CH-46 Sea Knight helicopters, MV-22 Osprey tilt-rotor aircraft, or AH-1 or UH-1 helicopters
Carrying capacity: 800 Marines

ABOVE: Amphibious warfare ships USSs *Carter Hall* (LSD 50) and *Iwo Jima* (LHD 7) steam off the coast of Liberia. The *Iwo Jima* Amphibious Ready Group was stationed there in support of peace-keeping efforts in the country's war-torn capital of Monrovia.
U.S. Navy photo by Photographer's Mate 3rd Class Julianne F. Metzger

RIGHT: Sailors man the rails aboard USS *Ogden* (LPD 5) as she pulls out of her berth at Naval Station San Diego, California. *Ogden* was deploying with Expeditionary Strike Group One (ESG-1) which had USS *Peleliu* (LHA 5) as flagship. An ESG is a naval strike force designed to equip amphibious forces with added firepower and operational capabilities.
U.S. Navy photo by Photographer's Mate 3rd Class Emmanuel Rios

Landing Craft Mechanized and Utility

These boats were developed to facilitate the U.S. island-hopping campaigns through the Pacific during World War II and are used to transport men, stores, and heavy equipment from ships lying offshore to beaches or port facilities. Their chief drawbacks are that they are slow, take time to load, and cannot move inland, unlike the navy's hovercraft-like LCUCs (landing craft utility cushion). Although the three classes of LCM (landing craft mechanized) and LCU (landing craft utility) perform the same role, the former carry smaller loads than the latter. The other main difference is that the LCMs have only a bow ramp to load and unload, which means they take longer to turn round, while the LCUs have a roll-on roll-off capability, with ramps both in the bow and stern, making them easier to load and unload.

Data: LCM Type 8
Length: 73 feet 7 inches
Displacement: 105 tons (full load)
Speed: 12 knots
Range: 190 miles at nine knots (full load)
Crew: Five
Carrying capacity: One M48 or one M60 tank; or 200 troops; or 180 tons of supplies

Data: LCM Type 6
Length: 56 feet 2 inches
Displacement: 64 tons (full load)
Speed: 9 knots
Range: 130 miles at nine knots (full load)
Crew: Five
Carrying capacity: 34 tons or 80 troops

Data: LCU 1610, 1627, and 1646 classes
Length: 134 feet 9 inches
Displacement: 375 tons (full load)
Speed: 11 knots
Range: 120 miles at eight knots (full load)
Crew: 14
Carrying capacity: 125 tons
Armament: Two 12.7 mm machine guns

BELOW: The amphibious assault ship USS *Essex* (LHD 2) launches LCUs. The *Essex* Amphibious Ready Group was off the coast of the Philippines to participate in Blue/Green Workups, a biannual joint training exercise with the 31st Marine Expeditionary Unit.
U.S. Navy photo by Journalist 2nd Class Wes Eplen

RIGHT: An LCU transports Marines and equipment of the 31st Marine Expeditionary Unit from USS *Essex* (LHD 2) to Subic Bay, Philippines.
U.S. Navy photo by Photographer's Mate Airman Marvin E. Thompson Jr.

LEFT: A local boy watches as *LCU 1631* approaches the beach to unload U.S. Marine Corps personnel and heavy equipment.
U.S. Navy photo by Photographer's Mate 2nd Class Andrew Meyers

RIGHT: Two photographs of LCACs docking in the well deck of the landing helicopter dock ship USS *Bataan* (LHD 5) as it prepares for its maiden deployment.
U.S. Navy photos by Photographer's Mate 3rd Class Dennis Timms (above) and Photographer's Mate 2nd Class Jimmy Lee

Landing Craft Air Cushion 1 Class

Conventional landing craft have two obvious shortcomings—they are limited to putting troops and equipment down on the shoreline and cannot move inland, and they are limited as to the type of beach on which they can operate: only an estimated 15 percent of potential landing sites are suited to their capabilities. The hovercraft-derived LCAC (landing craft air cushion) is an attempt to resolve these problems; they can move off the beaches and head inland, and are not stopped by offshore barriers such as coral reefs: indeed, they can reach 90 percent of the world's coastlines. They also have the advantage that they are faster than conventional landing craft and can therefore make the return ship-to-shore journey more quickly. The concept evolved along with the development of the Whidbey Bay class of LSDs (see page 192) in the 1980s, which were specifically built to operate air-cushioned vehicles, and the first LCACs were delivered in 1982. Construction work was earmarked for Textron Land and Marine Systems and Avondale Gulfport Marine and by 1986 some 33 units had been delivered. More followed over the following years—15 in the financial year 1989, and 12 more in 1990–1991; by 1995 the U.S. Navy had taken charge of 82 LCACs. They can transport troops, supplies, heavy weapons, and armored vehicles of between 60 and 75 tons. The LCACs are powered by four TF-40B gas turbines two of which are used for forward movement and two for lift.

Length: 87 feet 11 inches
Displacement: 87.2 tons (empty);170–182 tons (full load)
Speed: 40+ knots (full load)
Range: 2,000 miles at 40 knots (full load)
Crew: Five
Armament: Two 12.7 mm machine gun mounts for combination of M-2HB 0.5-caliber machine gun, Mk. 19 40 mm grenade-launcher, and M60 machine gun
Carrying capacity: Up to 24 troops or a single main battle tank

LEFT: Two CH-53 Super Stallions overfly an LCAC rushing toward the beach during an amphibious landing exercise in Kuwait conducted by the 15th Marine Expeditionary Unit and the USS *Bonhomme Richard* (LHD 6) Amphibious Ready Group.
U.S. Marine Corps photo courtesy of Gunnery Sargeant Glenn Holloway

RIGHT: An LCAC from Assault Craft Unit Five, Camp Pendleton, prepares to load Marines attached to the amphibious assault ship USS *Germantown* (LSD 42) as part of Cooperation Afloat Readiness and Training 2000, a bilateral exercise between U.S. naval forces and Southeast Asian navies.
U.S. Navy photo by Photographer's Mate 1st Class Spike Call

BELOW: An M1A1 Abrams embarks aboard a U.S. Navy LCAC at White Beach, Camp Pendleton, for transport to the amphibious transport dock ship USS *Comstock* (LSD 45) during Exercise Kernel Blitz '97.
U.S. Navy photo by Photographer's Mate Chief Robert Shanks

Whidbey Bay Class

This class of LSD (landing ship dock) grew out of the U.S. Navy's requirement for an amphibious assault ship that could land troops from helicopters as well as conventional and air-cushioned landing craft. The original design work for the named ship of the class, *Whidbey Bay* (LSD 41), started in the mid-1970s with the intention of replacing the eight ships of the ageing Thomaston class of LSDs as soon as possible, but attempts at cost-cutting by President Jimmy Carter delayed the program until 1981, when the go-ahead was finally given by President Ronald Reagan. Construction work was placed with Lockheed Shipbuilding of Seattle, Washington (LSDs 41–43) and Avondale Shipyards, New Orleans, Louisiana (LSDs 44–48). The *Whidbey Bay* was finally deployed on February 9, 1985. The units are powered by diesel engines rather that the previous steam turbines thereby making considerable savings on the cost of fuel and are also markedly different from similar earlier vessels in having a larger dock well that is capable of holding four LCACs (more than any other U.S. amphibious assault ship) and a larger flightdeck capable of accommodating the largest helicopters. The larger dock did reduce the ship's cargo-carrying capacity but it was thought that the top speed of the LCAC, which is around 50 knots and thus significantly greater than conventional landing craft, more than compensated for the reduction in storage space. Two helicopters at a time can use the ship's aft flightdeck. There are eight of the units in service and they are currently based at San Diego, California (3), Sasebo, Japan (1), and Little Creek, Virginia (4).

Length: 609 feet

Displacement: 15,939 tons (full load)

Speed: 20+ knots

Crew: 22 officers; 391 other ranks

Armament: Two Phalanx CIWSs; two Mk. 38 machine guns; six 0.5-caliber machine guns

Landing craft: Four LCACs

Carrying capacity: 504 Marines

OPPOSITE PAGE: USS *Comstock*, (LSD 45) anchors in the Eastern Channel of the Sitka Sound, Alaska, during Northern Edge 2000.
U.S. Air Force photo courtesy of Technical Sergeant Brian Snyder

LEFT: Aerial port bow view of the amphibious dock landing ship USS Oak Hill (LSD 51) underway during builder sea trials.
U.S. Navy photo courtesy Avondale Shipyards

INSET LEFT: USS *Ashland* (LSD 48) underway in the Mediterranean Sea while assigned to Amphibious Task Force East in support of Operation Enduring Freedom.
U.S. Navy photo by Photographer's Mate Airman Kenny Swartout

INSET RIGHT: A Marine CH-46 Sea Knight lands on board the dock landing ship USS *Fort McHenry* (LSD 43) during Exercise Tandem Thrust '97 in Australia.
U.S. Navy photo by Cpl Bryan P. Reed

Harpers Ferry Class

The Harpers Ferry class of LSD (landing ship dock) is effectively a modified version of the Whidbey Bay class. Indeed, the two types are are more or less 90 percent identical in all aspects of their look and layout. The principal difference lies in their cargo-carrying abilities. The former's is the greater and grew out of the U.S. Navy's single requests for what was officially known as an LSD 41 (Cargo Variant), which was made in 1987. The designers' response to the call was to reduce the number of LCACs from four on the Whidbey Bay units to two on the new LSDs and use the saved dock space for storing extra supplies. Construction work was undertaken by Louisiana-based Avondale Industries and the named ship of the class, the *Harpers Ferry* (LSD 49), was first deployed on January 7, 1995. Currently there are four of the units serving in the U.S. Navy and they are based at San Diego, California (1), Sasebo, Japan (1), and Little Creek, Virginia (2). As with the Whidbey Bay class the Harpers Ferry vessels (LSDs 49–52) are primarily used to transport Marine expeditionary units to hostile beaches and then land both them and their equipment by helicopter or landing craft. The ships have an aft flightdeck that can take two CH-53D Sea Stallion helicopters at any one time but have no hangars or maintenance facilities for the aircraft.

Length: 609 feet
Displacement: 16,708 tons (full load)
Speed: 20+ knots
Crew: 22 officers; 379 other ranks
Armament: Two Phalanx CIWSs; two Mk. 38 machine guns; six 0.5-caliber machine guns
Landing craft: Two LCACs
Carrying capacity: 504 Marines

LEFT: USS *Harpers Ferry* (LSD 49) sails at dusk off the coast of East Timor while providing medical and humanitarian assistance.
U.S. Navy photo by Photographer's Mate 3rd Class Joseph Tepas

RIGHT: USS *Comstock* (LSD 45) anchors at the mouth of the fjord-like entrance to Sawmill Bay in Sitka Sound, Alaska, during Northern Edge 2000.
U.S. Air Force photo courtesy of Technical Sergeant Brian Snyder

BELOW: USS *Harpers Ferry* cuts a path through the Arabian Gulf in support of Fifth Fleet operations.
U.S. Navy photo by Photographer's Mate 3rd Class Scott Richards

SEAPOWER | AMPHIBIOUS WARFARE VESSELS

194

Tarawa Class

The design for the Tarawa class of LHAs (landing helicopter assault) originated in the 1960s and the chief requirement was for a wholly new type of amphibious warfare warship that could undertake missions previously associated with a range of single-role vessels. What resulted from the U.S. Navy's requirements was a class over twice the size of any previous amphibious type, something akin to a conventional aircraft carrier of the time that also had both an aft docking well for landing craft and a large helicopter hangar. Construction of the LHAs, which was to be based on an advanced modular system, was given to Ingalls Shipbuilding of Pascagoula, Mississippi, and the named ship of the class, the *Tarawa* (LHA 1) was deployed on May 29, 1976. Eight further Tarawas were planned but the withdrawal of U.S. forces from the Vietnam War led to a reduction in requirements and four were canceled. The LHAs' primary role is to land Marine expeditionary units on enemy shores through the use of helicopters and both conventional and air-cushioned landing craft. However, they can also use their complement of Harriers and attack helicopters to directly support such landings and deploy some of their helicopters in the anti-submarine role. The final unit in the class, the *Peleliu* (LHA 5), was completed in 1980 and all five of the class are still in service today. All are named after renowned Marine Corps' battles from either World War I or World War II and they are currently based at San Diego, California (3), and Norfolk, Virginia (2).

Length: 820 feet

Displacement: 39,400 tons (full load)

Speed: 24 knots

Crew: 82 officers; 882 other ranks

Armament: Two RAM launchers; two Phalanx CIWSs; three 0.5-caliber machine guns; four Mk. 38 25 mm machine guns

Aircraft (mission dependent): Twelve CH-46 Sea Knight helicopters; four CH-53E Sea Stallion helicopters; six AV-8B Harrier attack aircraft; three UH-1N helicopters; four AH-1W Super Cobra helicopters

Carrying capacity: 1,900+ Marines

LEFT: An MV-22B Osprey (right) waits to launch off the flightdeck of the USS *Saipan* (LHA 2) during the aircraft's testing and evaluation trials. *U.S. Navy photo by Photographer's Mate 1st Class Tina M. Ackerman*

ABOVE RIGHT: U.S. Marines from the 15th MEU go ashore in Kuwait from amphibious assault ship USS *Tarawa* (LHA 1). *U.S. Navy photo by Photographer's Mate 3rd Class Taylor Goode*

ABOVE RIGHT: USSs *Nassau* (LHA 4) and *John F. Kennedy* (CV 67) moored in the Hudson River while participating in International Naval Review 2000 celebrations. *U.S. Navy photo by Photographer's Mate 1st Class Martin Maddock*

Wasp Class

The Wasp class of LHDs (landing helicopter dock) are the largest amphibious warfare warships currently in service anywhere in the world and are designed to conduct worldwide amphibious assaults against hostile shores by deploying Marine expeditionary units by helicopter and both conventional or air-cushioned landing craft, and supporting their initial landings. In addition, some of their helicopters can act in the anti-submarine warfare role. Construction of the Wasp LHDs was given to Northrop Grumman Ship Systems Ingalls Operations of Pascagoula, Mississippi, and the named ship of the class, the *Wasp* (LHD 1) was commissioned at Norfolk, Virginia, on July 29, 1989. To fulfill their various roles the Wasp-class vessels have a large aft docking well that can take up to three air-cushioned assault craft and a large hangar that gives access to the flightdeck by way of two elevators, one situated starboard, aft of the island superstructure, and the other on the port side amidships. The LHDs also have a formidable storage capacity that can accommodate a mix of up to five main battle tanks, 25 LAV-25 armored personnel carriers, eight 155 mm howitzers, 68 trucks, and 10 logistics vehicles. There are currently seven Wasp class LHDs in service; they have their home ports in San Diego, California (2), Sasebo, Japan (1), and Norfolk, Virginia (4). The eighth vessel of the Tarawa design will be the *Makin Island* (LHD 8). The contract for this unit was issued in April 2002 and the scheduled delivery date is July 31, 2007.

Length: 844 feet

Displacement (full load): 40,650 tons (LHDs 1–4); 40,358 tons (LHDs 5–7), 41,772 tons (LHD 8)

Speed: 20+ knots

Crew: 104 officers; 1,004 other ranks

Armament: Two RAM launchers; two NATO Sea Sparrow launchers; two (LHDs 5–7) or three (LHDs 1–4) Phalanx CIWSs; four 0.5-caliber MGs; two (LHDs 1–4) or three (LHDs 5–7) Mk. 38 25 mm MGs

Aircraft (mission dependent): Twelve CH-46 Sea Knight helicopters; four CH-53E Sea Stallion helicopters; six AV-8B Harrier attack aircraft; three UH-1N Huey helicopters; four AH-1W Super Cobra helicopters

Carrying capacity: 1,894 Marines

LEFT: USS *Kearsarge* (LHD 3) turns into the wind to recover aircraft.
U.S. Navy photo by Chief Warrant Officer 2 Seth Rossman

RIGHT: USS *Essex* (LHD 2) leads its Amphibious Readiness Group—USS *Juneau* (LPD 10), USS *Germantown* (LSD 42), and USS *Fort McHenry* (LSD 43) with the 31st Marine Expeditionary Unit (MEU) embarked—during exercise "Blue-Green Workups."
U.S. Navy photo by Photographer's Mate Airman Apprentice Stephanie M. Bergman

FAR RIGHT: USS *Wasp* (LHD 1) off the coast of Greece near Litokohoron Beach with Mount Olympus in the background.
U.S. Navy photo by Photographer's Mate 1st Class Phil Pruitt

BOTTOM RIGHT: USS *Kearsarge* (LHD-3) anchored in the Persian Gulf while conducting a Marine offload. *Kearsarge* was deployed as the flagship of Amphibious Task Force East in support of Operation Enduring Freedom.
U.S. Navy photo by Photographer's Mate Airman Kenny Swartout

Amphibious Assault Vehicles

The AAV currently employed by the U.S. Marine Corps is the LVTP 7 that entered service in the 1970s but underwent a name change—and little else—to AAVP 7A1 (Amphibious Assault Vehicle Personnel 7A1) in 1985. The AAV 7A1 is an armored, tracked assault vehicle designed to transport Marines from ship to shore and them move them inland. As it is armed, it can perform the same function on land as the army's M2A1 Bradley infantry fighting vehicle, although its thinner armor and weaker armament makes it much more vulnerable to enemy fire. It can also perform as a cargo carrier and ambulance. As the AAVP 7A1 is essentially a vehicle from the late 1960s–early 1970s, it will need replacing despite the implementation of a service life extension program completed in 1986. The program has been dogged by problems, and the new Advanced AAV is not likely to enter production before 2006, with full operational capacity not being reached for a further twelve years. The Marines require more than a thousand of the new AAVs at an estimated cost of around $7 billion.

Data: AAVP 7A1

Weight: 50.758 lb combat-loaded; 56,743 lb troop-loaded; 60,758 lb cargo-loaded

Speed: 20–30 mph on land; six mph at sea

Range: 300 miles on land at 25 mph; seven hours' endurance at sea

Crew: Three

Armament: One Mk. 19 40 mm MG; one 0.5-caliber MG

Carrying capacity: 21 combat equipped troops or 10,000 lb of cargo

Data: Advanced AAV

Weight: 62,880 lb empty; 74,500 lb with fuel, ammunition, troops, and crew

Speed: 45 mph on land; 25 knots on water (maximum)

Range: 300 miles at 25 mph on land; 65 nautical miles at 20 knots at sea

Crew: Three

Armament: One Bushmaster II 30 mm cannon; one M240 7.62 mm MG

Carrying capacity: 17 combat-equipped troops

BELOW INSET: U.S. and Korean forces conduct an amphibious landing at Tok So Ri beach near Pohang, S. Korea during Exercise Foal Eagle 2000.
U.S. Navy photo by Captain Donald P. Cook

LEFT: AAVs from USSs *Whidbey Island* (LSD 41) and *Shreveport* (LPD 12) rush the beach during an exercise off the coast of North Carolina.
U.S. Navy photo by Photographer's Mate 3rd Class M. Dennis Timms

RIGHT: The Auxiliary Command Ship USS *Coronado* (AGF 11) heads back to sea during Exercise RIMPAC '98, a large multi-national maritime exercise in the Pacific.
U.S. Navy photo by Photographer's Mate 2nd Class August Sigur

La Salle class

The single ship of the La Salle Class is designated as the AGF 3 and is currently configured as one of the U.S. Navy's command ships. However, the *La Salle* began life earmarked as the final unit of the three-ship Raleigh class of LPDs (landing craft dock) that entered service between 1962 and 1963. As the LPD 3, the original vessel was constructed by the New York Navy Shipyard to deploy amphibious assault forces against hostile shores by landing craft and helicopters, thereby doing away with the need to have several specialist vessels to undertake individual missions as had previously been the case. *La Salle* was subsequently converted to its present command-and-control role by the Philadelphia Navy Yard, Pennsylvania, and was redesignated. The bulk of the conversion involved building accommodation and work space for fleet commanders and their staff, as well as installing the appropriate radar arrays and command-and-control systems. The *La Salle* carries only defensive armaments based on the Phalanx CIWS, chaff dispensers to decoy incoming missiles, and various mounts for machine guns. It also has a helicopter platform for deploying and retrieving such aircraft and normally carries one helicopter as standard. At present the *La Salle* is the flagship of the commander of the U.S. Sixth Fleet, which usually operates in the Mediterranean but it has also been deployed to the Indian Ocean on several occasions in the recent past. Its home base is normally Gaeta, Italy.

Length: 520 feet
Displacement: 14,650 tons (full load)
Speed: 20 knots
Crew: 440 officers and crew with 59 flag staff
Armament: Two Phalanx CIWSs; four MG mounts; two saluting guns
Aircraft: A single light helicopter

Coronado class

The single ship of this class, the *Coronado* (AGF 11), began life as one of the Austin class of LPDs that was completed between the mid-1960s and early 1970s by Lockheed Shipbuilding and Construction to replace the U.S. Navy's ageing fleet of Raleigh-class LPDs. The *Coronado* was designated LPD 11 but in October 1980 was ordered to undergo modification to become an AGF to temporarily replace the *La Salle* (AGF 3), which was undergoing a refit. The changes to the *Coronado* were undertaken by the Philadelphia Navy Yard, Pennsylvania. Today the AGF is configured to offer communication systems and accommodation for fleet commanders and their staff. AGF II is not a combat ship as such and is armed with defensive weapons systems, including the Phalanx CIWS, air and surface radars, chaff launchers, and various electronic warfare arrays. Like the *La Salle*, the *Coronado* is deployed as a flagship—that of the Third Fleet, which operates in the Pacific. It home port is San Diego, California.

Length: 570 feet
Displacement: 16,912 tons (full load)
Speed: 21 knots
Crew: 516 officers and crew with 120 flag staff
Armament: Two Phalanx CIWSs; two 12.7 mm MGs
Aircraft: Two light helicopters

Other Vessels

Although large fighting warships are the cornerstone of any modern navy, the complex nature of maritime warfare requires that they be supported by a wide range of smaller vessels. These fall into several categories and include: mine countermeasures ships, small patrol craft for work along coastlines and inland waterways; and a number of large combat-support ships that service warships by providing them with the stores—from fuel and ammunition to food—that allow them to remain on station. The U.S. Navy also has its own special forces and these have been provided with small craft that can insert teams into combat zones and then extract them. Two other types of vessel are also covered in this section—recovery and salvage types and those dedicated to research.

RIGHT: Joint Venture, High Speed Vessel Experimental One (HSV X1) during Operation Iraqi Freedom.
U.S. Navy photo by Photographer's Mate 2nd Class (AW) Michael J. Pusnik Jr.

INSET: USS *Blue Ridge* (LCC 19) comes alongside USNS *Pecos* (T-AO 197), to take on fuel during an RAS while en route to its homeport of Yokosuka, Japan.
U.S. Navy photo by Photographer's Mate 2nd Class Clinton C. Beaird

LEFT: The coastal mine-hunters USS *Cardinal* (MHC 60), left, and USS *Raven* (MHC 61) rest above the submerged deck of the commercial motor vessel *Blue Marlin* prior to deballasting operations that would lift the mine-hunters onto *Blue Marlin*'s deck (see also photo on page 229 for a month-long transit to the Arabian.
U.S. Navy photo by Lt G Chuck Bell

Deep Submergence Rescue Vehicles

The U.S. Navy's need for deep submergence rescue vehicles (DSRVs) was revealed by the loss of the submarine USS *Thresher* and all of its crew in 1963. The overwhelming problem was that submarines of the time could dive deeper than any rescue submersibles then available. Consequently the navy authorized the Deep Submergence Systems Project and development work begin in conjunction with Lockheed Missile and Space. The first of two deep-diving submersibles, the USS *Mystic* (DSRV 1), was launched in 1970 and was followed by the USS *Avalon* (DSRV 2). The DSRVs can be transported quickly to any incident by large truck, aircraft, ship, or on the upper surface of the hull of modified attack submarine. Once over an accident site the DSRVs are deployed from either a suitable surface ship or the submarine. They are able to dive to great depths, conduct sonar searches to locate a target, and have a docking system that allows them to attach themselves to a disabled submarine's hatches to permit the escape of its crew in batches of 24. To facilitate any rescue the DSRVs are fitted with an arm to clear debris and obstructions that might be blocking a hatch, and a combined cable-cutter and gripper that is able to lift some 1,000 lb. Although the DSRVs are primarily tasked to aid U.S. Navy submarines, they can, if deemed appropriate by the government, go to the aid of foreign vessels.

Length: 49 feet

Displacement: 38 tons

Speed: Four knots

Crew: Two pilots and two rescue crew

Maximum diving depth: 5,000 feet

Passengers: 24 (maximum)

ABOVE: The U.S. Navy Los Angeles-class submarine USS *La Jolla* (SSN 701)—with the deep submergence rescue vehicle *Mystic* (DSRV-1) attached—is escorted by the Japanese Coast Guard as it pulls out of Sasebo harbor to participate in the submarine rescue exercise Pacific Reach 2002.
U.S. Navy photo by Journalist 3rd Class Wes Eplen

Military Sealift Command

ABOVE: HMAS *Success* (AOR 304) steams alongside USS *Essex* (LHD 2) for an underway replenishment. *Success* transferred over 330,000 gallons of various fuels to *Essex* while both ships crossed the equator. *U.S. Navy photo by Photographer's Mate Airman Recruit Stephanie M. Bergman*

The U.S. Navy does not directly operate many logistic and support vessels, leaving this side of naval operations to an organization known as the Military Sealift Command (MSC), whose ships are unarmed and largely crewed by civilians. They are are usually known as United States Naval Ships (USNSs). Under normal conditions, the MSC operates worldwide around 70 ships, mostly tankers and various types of cargo vessels, but this can be increased during periods of crisis. The MSC has four main areas of responsibility. First, prepositioning—placing and maintaining ships containing equipment for the Marines, air force, navy, and army close to potential crisis areas worldwide. The main bases are in the Mediterranean, and at Diego Garcia in the Indian Ocean, and at Guam in the Pacific. Second, surge sealift—these vessels are mostly stationed in the continental United States and are used to deploy heavy equipment worldwide in the event of a crisis. Third, special mission ships, which comprise specialist vessels that can each undertake a particular mission, from cable-laying and repair, through oceanic survey and surveillance. Fourth, the Naval Fleet Auxiliary Force (NFAF), which can directly support military operations. The NFAF includes hospital ships, fast combat support ships, combat stores ships, tugs, and replenishment oilers. Although the MSC is the backbone of U.S. military overseas logistical support, the U.S. Navy does have its own small fleet of such vessels, including the *Mount Hood* (AE 29), a Kiluauea class ammunition ship; the Supply and Sacramento classes of Fast Combat Support Ships (AOEs); and nuclear submarine tenders of the L. Y. Spear class, which are designated AS.

Continued on page 206.

THIS PAGE: USNS *Walter S. Diehl* (T-AO 193) pulls alongside
USS *Nimitz* (CVN 68), preparing for an underway replenishment
U.S. Navy photo by Photographer's Mate 3rd Class Yesenia Rosas

RIGHT: USS *Seattle* receives fuel from the Japanese fleet support ship
Tokiwa (AOE 423).
U.S. Navy photo by Photographer's Mate 1st Class Jim Hampshire

Data: Kiluauea Class AEs
Length: 564 feet
Displacement: 18,088 tons (full load)
Speed: 20+ knots
Crew: 17 officers; 366 other ranks
Armament: Two Phalanx CIWSs
Aircraft: Two CH-46 Sea Knight helicopters

Data: Supply Class AOEs
Length: 754 feet
Displacement: 48,800 tons (full load)
Speed: 25 knots
Crew: 40 officers; 627 other ranks
Armament: Two Phalanx CIWSs; Nato Sea Sparrow
SAMs; two 25 mm machine guns
Aircraft: Three CH-46 Sea Knight helicopters

Data: Sacramento Class AOEs
Length: 793 feet
Displacement: 53,000 tons (full load)
Speed: 26 knots
Crew: 24 officers/576 other ranks
Armament: Two Phalanx CIWSs; Nato Sea Sparrow
SAMs
Aircraft: Three CH-46 Sea Knight helicopters

Data: L. Y. Spear Class ASs
Length: 644 feet
Displacement: 23,493 tons (full load)
Speed: 20 knots
Crew: 97 officers; 1266 other ranks
Armament: Two 40 mm guns; four 20 mm guns

ABOVE: An aviation ordnanceman mans his watch station at the 20 mm chain gun on board USS *Peleliu* (LHA 5) as the fast combat support ship *Sacramento* (AOE 1) delivers fuel and supplies. The Ticonderoga-class guided missile cruiser USS *Philippine Sea* (CG 58) is seen in the background providing air cover and protection for the two ships conducting the RAS. The three ships were operating together as part of Operation Enduring Freedom.
U.S. Navy photo by Master Chief Photographer's Mate Terry Cosgrove

RIGHT: At sea with the *John C. Stennis* Battle Group. The U.S. Navy auxiliary supply ship USS *Bridge* (AOE 10) leads (from right) USS *Elliot* (DD 967), Canadian Navy ship HMCS *Vancouver* (CPF 331), and U.S. Navy guided missile cruiser USS *Port Royal* (CG 73) as they join together to conduct operations in support of Operation Enduring Freedom.
U.S. Navy photo by Photographer's Mate 3rd Class Margaret M. Taylor

RIGHT: A CH-46 Sea Knight helicopter assigned to the "Dragon Whales" of Helicopter Combat Support Squadron HC-8 attached to the fast combat support ship USS *Detroit* (AOE 4) assists in the turn over of deployment responsibilities between USS *John F. Kennedy* (CV 67) and USS *Theodore Roosevelt* (CVN 71) in the Red Sea. *Roosevelt* was returning home.
U.S. Navy photo by Chief Photographer's Mate Eric A. Clement

FAR RIGHT: Another photograph taken as USS *Sacramento* (AOE 1), foreground, delivers fuel and supplies to USS *Peleliu* with USS *Philippine Sea* (CG 58) watchful in the background during Operation Enduring Freedom.
U.S. Navy Photo by Master Chief Photographer's Mate Terry Cosgrove

FAR LEFT: Boatswain's Mate 2nd Class Bobby Nelson from Linden, Michigan, directs from the hangar bay of USS *Theodore Roosevelt* (CVN 71) during an underway replenishment with USS *Arctic* (AOE 8) in the Adriatic Sea.
U.S. Navy photo by Photographer's Mate Airman Apprentice Charles Thompson

LEFT: Sailors aboard USS *Enterprise* (CVN 65) watch from the hangar bay doors during an underway replenishment with USS *Detroit* (AOE 4) in the Persian Gulf.
U.S. Navy photo by Photographer's Mate Second Class John Mahoney

ABOVE: RAS between USS *Blue Ridge* (LCC 19) and USNS *Pecos* (T-AO 197).
U.S. Navy photo by Photographer's Mate 2nd Class Clinton C. Beaird

FOLLOWING PAGES (212/213):
PAGE 212: USS *Enterprise* (CVN 65) and the auxiliary oiler USS *Monongahela* (AO 178) conduct an RAS in the Mediterranean.
U.S. Photo by Photographer's Mate 3rd Class Jason D. Malcom

PAGE 213: Amber lights illuminate the deck of the fast combat support ship USS *Detroit* (AOE 4) during an early morning underway replenishment with USS *Enterprise* (CVN 65).
U.S. Navy photo by Photographer's Mate 3rd Class Shelton T. Young

RIGHT: Sailors aboard the fast combat support ship USS *Sacramento* (AOE 1) work to maintain control of the lines in high winds and heavy seas during an underway replenishment with the aircraft carrier *Carl Vinson* in the Pacific Ocean.
U.S. Navy photo by Photographer's Mate Airman Dustin Howell

FAR RIGHT: MSC oiler USNS *Big Horn* (TAO 198) and the destroyer USS *Spruance* (DD 963) are framed in the pilot house windows aboard the *La Salle* (AGF 3).
U.S. Navy photo by Todd Reeves

RIGHT: Quartermaster Seaman Apprentice Lauren Williams of Rhode Island, N.Y., signals the USNS *Rappahannock* (T-AO 204) showing her relative position in relation to the tip of USS *Kitty Hawk*'s flightdeck during Exercise Keen Sword 2003. Keen Sword 2003 was the seventh in a series of regularly scheduled exercises involving the Japanese Maritime Self-Defense Force.
U.S. Navy photo by Photographer's Mate 1st Class Ted Banks

FAR RIGHT: The guided-missile cruiser USS *Hue City* (CG 66) steams alongside the fast combat support ship USS *Seattle* (AOE 3) during an underway replenishment at sea.
U.S. Navy photo by Chief Photographer's Mate Spike Call

LEFT: During a replenishment at sea with USNS *Rappahannock* (T-AO 204), gunner's mates fire tending lines to the crew aboard the replenishment ship from the hangar bay aboard USS *Kitty Hawk* (CV 63).
U.S. Navy photo by Photographer's Mate Airman Mara McCleaft

RIGHT: The MSC oiler USNS *Kanawha* (T-AO 196) moves fuel lines across pulleys to begin an underway replenishment with USS *Ronald Reagan* (CVN 76).
U.S. Navy photo by Photographer's Mate Airman Kyle L. O'Neill

FOLLOWING PAGES (220/221):
PAGE 220: The MSC oiler USNS *Kanawha* (T-AO 196) pulls alongside USS *Theodore Roosevelt* (CVN 71) for a RAS.
U.S. Navy photo by Photographer's Mate Airman Tony C. Foster

PAGE 221: USNS *John Lenthall* (T-AO 189) steams away from USS *Enterprise* (CVN 65) after completing an early-morning VERTREP.
U.S. Navy photo by Photographer's Mate Airman Rob Gaston

RIGHT: Fuel lines are passed from USS *Peleliu* (LHA 5) over to USS *Jarrett* (FFG 33) during an underway replenishment in the Indian Ocean.
U.S. Navy photo by Photographer's Mate 2nd Class Joshua L. Pritekel

FAR RIGHT: USNS *Supply* (T-AOE 6) steams alongside USS *Enterprise* (CVN 65) while conducting an early morning RAS in the Atlantic Ocean.
U.S. Navy photo by Photographer's Mate Airman Rob Gaston

THIS PAGE AND RIGHT: Two views of USNS *Sgt. 1st Class Randall D. Shughart* (T-AKR 295), one of nineteen fast (20+ knots) maritime prepositioning ships built or converted to maintain army brigade equipment sets close to potential conflict zones. The *Shughart* is named for an Army Special Forces sniper and Medal of Honor winner killed in Somalia in 1993. The *Shughart* and her sisters are equipped with heavy roll-on/roll-off ramps, for rapid loading and unloading of vehicles and cargo. *Official U. S. Navy photos*

ABOVE: The mine countermeasure ship USS *Dextrous* (MCM 13) takes part in mine countermeasure operations in the Arabian Gulf along with coalition forces.
U.S. Navy photo by Photographer's Mate 1st Class Brien Aho

LEFT: Aviation Ordnanceman 1st Class David Ahearn (the diver) attaches an inert satchel charge to a training mine, during exercises in waters off Naval Base Guantanamo Bay, Cuba.
U.S. Navy Photograph by Photographer's Mate 2nd Class Andrew Mckaskle

RIGHT: The coastal mine-hunters USS *Cardinal* (MHC 60, left) and USS *Raven* (MHC 61) rest on the deck of the commercial motor vessel *Blue Marlin* at Ingleside, Texas.
U.S. Navy photo by Lt (JG) Chuck Bell

Osprey class

During the 1980s the U.S. Navy began to overhaul and modernize its mine countermeasures force, focusing on creating a new generation of minesweeping helicopters and two new classes of minesweepers, the first large mine countermeasures vessels to be built in the United States for nearly 30 years. One of the new minesweepers was designated the Osprey class of coastal mine hunters (MHCs). They deploy conventional sweeping measures along with capable cutters and a detonating device that can be exploded by remote control to neutralize moored and bottom mines. Sonar and video systems are used to locate potential targets. The contract to build the new class was given to manufacturers Intermarine USA based in Savannah, Georgia (MHCs 51, 52, 55, and 58–61), and Avondale Industries of Gulfport, Mississippi (MHC 53, 54, 56, and 57). The named ship of the class, the USS *Osprey* (MHC 51), was deployed on November 20, 1993, and like its sister ships, its hull is built from glass-reinforced plastic. Today the U.S. Navy has twelve Osprey Class MHCs in service, ten of which have their home base at Ingleside, Texas (MHCs 51–59 and 62); the other two are deployed overseas. Both the USS *Cardinal* (MHC 60) and the USS *Raven* (MHC 61) sail out of Manama, Bahrain, reflecting the ongoing instability within the Middle East and Persian Gulf. All of the MHCs can operate for a maximum of fifteen days before needing replenishment from a support ship or shore base.

Length: 188 feet
Displacement: 893 tons (full load)
Speed: 10+ knots
Crew: 5 officers; 46 other ranks
Armament: Two 0.5-caliber machine guns

RIGHT: K-Dog, a bottlenose dolphin belonging to Commander Task Unit (CTU) 55.4.3, leaps out of the water in front of Marine Sergeant Andrew Garrett while training near the landing dock ship USS *Gunston Hall* (LSD 44) in the Arabian Gulf. Attached to the dolphin's pectoral fin is a "pinger" device that allows the handler to keep track of the dolphin when out of sight. CTU 55.4.3 is a multinational team consisting of Naval Special Clearance Team One, Fleet Diving Unit Three from the United Kingdom, Clearance Dive Team from Australia, and Explosive Ordnance Disposal Mobile Units Six and Eight. The team was conducting deep/shallow water mine countermeasure operations to clear shipping lanes for humanitarian relief when this photograph was taken.
U.S. Navy photo by Photographer's Mate 1st Class Brien Aho

FAR RIGHT: The MSC missile-range instrumentation ship USNS *Observation Island* (T-AGM 23) lies tied up at Naval Station, Pearl Harbor. *Observation Island* has provided a testbed for numerous U.S. Navy weapons systems over the decades.
U.S. Navy photo by Operations Specialist 2nd Class John Bouvia

Avenger class

Along with minehunting helicopters and the Osprey class of MHC, the concept of the Avenger class of ocean-going mine hunter-killer vessels grew out of the U.S. Navy's decision in the early 1980s to overhaul its increasingly outdated mine countermeasures force. The need for this overhaul became increasingly clear during that decade's Iran–Iraq War in which the Persian Gulf was sown with mines that threatened the flow of oil to the West. Construction work on the new class of MCMs was given to two companies—Peterson Shipbuilders of Sturgeon Bay, Wisconsin, and Marinette Marine of Marinette, Wisconsin. The MCMs have a wooden hull sheathed in fiberglass and are equipped with sonar and video arrays to detect mines that can be neutralized by convention means—cable-cutters and remotely detonated devices. The name ship of the class, the USS *Avenger* (MCM 1), was deployed on September 12, 1983, and a further thirteen ships followed, with the final batch of three being purchased in 1990. The overwhelming bulk of the ships are based at Ingleside, Texas (MCMs 1–4, 6, 8–11, and 14), which is also the main base for the MHCs. Four Avengers normally serve overseas: the USSs *Guardian* (MCM 5) and *Patriot* (MCM 7) are based at Sasebo, Japan, while the USSs *Ardent* (MCM 12) and *Dextrous* (MCM 13) have been forward-deployed to Manama, Bahrain, in the Persian Gulf. Two of the MCMs, the *Avenger* and *Guardian*, played a prominent role in naval operations during Operations Desert Shield and Desert Storm during 1990 and 1991.

Length: 224 feet
Displacement: 1,312 tons (full load)
Speed: 14 knots
Crew: 8 officers; 76 other ranks
Armament: Two 0.5-caliber machine guns

RIGHT: Deck personnel transfer cargo from MSC fleet auxiliary ammunition ship USNS *Mount Baker* (T-AE 34), while ordnance is airlifted simultaneously by helicopter to USS *Harry S. Truman*'s flightdeck.
U.S. Navy photo by Photographer's Mate Airman Ryan O'Connor

Left: Naval Special Warfare (NSW) 11-Meter Rigid-Hull Inflatable Boats (RHIBs) operated by Special Boat Unit 20 approaches USS *Shreveport* (LPD 12) to pick up SEALs. *U.S. Navy Photo by Photographer's Mate 2nd Class David C. Mercil*

Right: A Humvee of the 1st Calvary Division, Fort Hood, Texas, rolls off USNS *Soderman* (T-AKR 299). *U.S. Navy photo by Staff Sergeant Lisa M. Zunzanyika-Carpenter*

Cyclone Class

At present the U.S. Navy operates just one type of patrol coastal ship (PC), the Cyclone class. The vessels were designed to undertake two types of mission: to directly protect the coastline, coastal waters, ports, and waterways of the continental United States, and to undertake surveillance tasks. In these roles the U.S. Navy PCs have worked in conjunction with the U.S. Coast Guard during anti-drug and counter-terrorist patrols. The Cyclone class was based on the six-strong Ramadan class of patrol craft built by Britain's Vosper Thornycroft for service with the Egyptian Navy, although the U.S. class has a markedly different appearance. It has a greater displacement, is longer, and has a greater range (2,500 miles at 12 knots as opposed to 1,600 miles at 18 knots). The U.S. Navy also required that the superstructure of the Cyclones be fitted with armor one-inch thick. Construction work in the United States was undertaken by Bollinger Shipyards, which has built fourteen of the vessels, all of which are named after strong winds. However, the named ship of the class, the *Cyclone* (PC 1), is no longer operating with the navy and was taken over by the Coast Guard on February 28, 2000. The remaining vessels are based at the Naval Amphibious Base, Little Creek, Virginia (nine—PCs 2, 5, 6, 9–15) and San Diego, California (four—PCs 3,4, 7, and 8). All of these PCs are under the direct control of the commander of Naval Special Forces.

Length: 170 feet

Displacement: 331 tons (full load)

Speed: 35 knots

Crew: 4 officers; 24 other ranks

Armament: One Mk. 96 25 mm MG; one Mk. 38 25 mm MG; five 0.5-caliber MGs, two Mk. 19 40 mm grenade-launchers; two M60 MGs

LEFT: The coastal patrol craft
USSs *Zephyr* (PC 8, back left),
Squall (PC 7, back right),
Monsoon (PC 4, (front left), and
Hurricane (PC 3, front right)
docked at San Diego Naval
Station, California.
*U.S. Navy photo by Photographer's
Mate 2nd Class Ted Banks*

FAR LEFT: An HH-60H Sea
Hawk from the "Red Wolves"—
Helicopter Combat Search and
Rescue/Special Warfare
Support Squadron HCS-4—is
used as a platform for deploying
SEAL team members onto a
Mk. V assault craft.
*U.S. Navy photo by Photographer's
Mate Chief Johnny R. Wilson*

RIGHT: The Norfolk-based salvage rescue ship USS *Grapple* (ARS 53) during acceptance trials.
U.S. Navy photo

THIS PICTURE: The U.S. Navy hospital ship USNS *Comfort* (T-AH 20) passes the Statue of Liberty en route to Manhattan to provide assistance to the victims of the September 11, 2001, terrorist attack on the World Trade Center.
U.S. Navy photo by Journalist 1st Class Preston Keres.

INSET LEFT: Quartermaster 1st Class Cass Shuschuller dons his fire-fighting ensemble while conducting fire-fighting drills aboard the auxiliary rescue salvage ship USS *Grasp* (ARS 51).
U.S. Navy photo by Photographer's Mate 1st Class Andrew McKaskle

Safeguard Class

The Safeguard class of ARS (accident recovery ships) was developed to support and then replace three Edenton-class types that were built in the 1970s and finally withdrawn from service in 1996. The Safeguard ARSs have four main maritime missions—to refloat stranded vessels, to lift loads from the ocean depths, to tow disabled vessels to safety, and to undertake manned diving operations to depths of up to 190 feet. They also have a firefighting capability thanks to fire monitors positioned forward and amidships that can use both sea water and foam to deal with any blaze and have storage holds containing equipment to assist in pumping out water, patching hulls, and generating electricity. The named ship of the four-vessel class, the USS *Safeguard* (ARS 50) was launched on August 16, 1985, and like the other ARSs in the class was built by Peterson Builders. All have a rugged all-steel hull, a range of around 8,000 miles at eight knots, and their primary lift gear comprises a forward boom of 7.5-ton capacity and an aft boom of 40-ton capacity. The vessels are normally based at Pearl Harbor, Hawaii (2), and Little Creek, Virginia (2). Although the Safeguard class is primarily responsible for the recovery and salvage of U.S. Navy and government ships on a worldwide basis, they have also assisted in such missions when foreign-owned vessels are involved, when it was considered appropriate to U.S. interests. In recent years the ARSs have also taken part in the recovery of aircraft that have crashed at sea.

Length: 255 feet
Displacement: 3282 tons (full load)
Speed: 14 knots
Crew: 6 officers; 94 other ranks
Armament: Two 0.5-caliber MGs; two Mk. 38 25 mm guns

Rigid Hull Inflatable Boats

Among the smallest craft in service with the U.S. Navy, rigid hull inflatable boats (RHIBs) are chiefly used for the insertion and extraction of small special force groups—chiefly SEAL teams—onto or off hostile shores. For this type of operation the chief requirements are for speed and a measure of all-weather capability. The RHIBs are powered by a Dual Caterpillar 3126 DITA turbocharged and aftercooled six in-line diesel engine and have a maximum speed of around 40 knots. To aid their sea-going abilities, the RHIBs are built from composite materials and an inflatable tube gunwale constructed out of reinforced fabric, thereby greatly increasing their buoyancy. They are built to withstand some of the roughest seas and can cope with wind speeds of up to 45 knots, although the navy has deemed that they cannot operate effectively on actual combat missions in wind speeds above 34 knots. Nevertheless, it has permitted them to function in speeds above 34 knots during training exercises. RHIBs can be deployed from a variety of larger warships, and are particularly associated with various amphibious warfare vessels. They have a maximum range of some 200 nautical miles, which gives their mother ships an excellent stand-off distance from the inflatables' targets. although mainly deployed on clandestine SEAL operations, RHIBs have also been seen service as riverine and coastal patrol vessels and are particularly suited to inland waterways that are often two narrow or shallow to accommodate larger craft.

Length: 35 feet 11 inches
Displacement: 17,400 lb (full load)
Speed: 40+ knots
Crew: Three
Armament: One 7.62 mm M60 MG; one M2 0.5-caliber MG; one Mk. 19 40 mm automatic grenade-launcher
Carrying capacity: One SEAL squad

Yard Patrol Craft

The U.S. Navy operates three classes of yard patrol craft (YPs), the YP 654, YP 676, and YP 696 classes. The YP 676s, and YP 696s are virtually identical and larger than the YP 654s. All of the types are tasked with training and research missions. In the former case the YPs mostly operate at the U.S. Naval Academy at Annapolis, Maryland, and at the Officer Candidate School, Pensacola, Florida. They are used to teach midshipmen and officer candidates maritime skills, basic damage-control skills, and navigation techniques. YPs are also operated by the Naval Undersea Warfare Center Division, which is based at Keyport, Washington. At this facility they fulfill a number of research functions from measuring underwater target and torpedo noise, to deploying static acoustic targets during torpedo testing and instruments to access sea water conductivity and temperature. The YP 654s were built by Stephens Brothers and Elizabeth City Systems, while the YP 676 and YP 696 classes were manufactured by Peterson Builders and Marinette Marine. All of the vessels have wooden hulls, aluminum superstructures, and 12V-71N Detroit diesel engines that drive two propellers. Although all have a maximum range of around 1,800 nautical miles, under optimum conditions they can travel a distance of 1,400 nautical miles at 12 knots in five days without taking on fuel.

Data: YP 654 Class
Length: 81 feet
Displacement: 66 tons (full load)
Speed: 12 knots
Range: 1,800 nautical miles (maximum)
Crew: 2 officers; 8 other ranks
Carrying capacity: 50 people (maximum)

Data: YP 676 and YP 696 classes
Length: 108 feet
Displacement:
Speed: 12+ knots
Range: 1800 nautical miles (maximum)
Crew: 2 officers; 4 other ranks
Carrying capacity: 50 people (maximum)

Mk. V Special Operations Craft

These fast, lightweight, boats have been design to insert and extract U.S. special forces into environments that are considered to offer a low to medium threat to any troops conducting clandestine missions. The project to acquire the Mk. V was overseen by the U.S. Special Operations Command's Special Operations Acquisition Executive and after agreeing the initial construction contracts, it took just eighteen months to deliver the first of the craft. The Mk. Vs are mostly deployed by U.S. Navy SEAL teams and are one of many specialist craft attached to the Naval Special Warfare Special Boat Squadron. They can be deployed anywhere in the world at short notice and can be transported into an area of operations by cargo aircraft, amphibious assault ships, and under their own power if located at a shore base in the vicinity of their target. Under normal circumstances the Mk. Vs are organized into sections each comprising two craft, their crews, and support elements. These detachments are on standby to move at no more that 48 hours' notice and once in theater are expected to be operational no more than 24 hours after arriving at their destination. In action they can be based at shore facilities, on deck-equipped ships, or surface vessels with appropriate cranes and sufficient deck storage space. Aside from their insertion-extraction role, the craft can also be deployed to undertake more routine patrol, surveillance, and interdiction work along coastlines and inland waterways.

Length: 82 feet
Displacement: 57 tons
Speed: 50 knots

RIGHT: A stern view of USS *Safeguard* (ARS 50), the U.S. Navy's only forward-deployed rescue and salvage ship, in dry dock for extensive repairs and maintenance. *U.S. Navy Photo by Photographer's Mate 1st Class Marvin Harris.*

Research Vessels

The U.S. Navy has a number of unarmed surface and underwater ships, both manned and unmanned, to undertake oceanic research and conduct evaluation trials on new equipment. The NR 1 Deep Submergence Craft is tasked with conducting deep-sea geological surveys, seafloor mapping, search and recovery missions, and the installation of underwater equipment. Although capable of staying on station for long periods, it has to be towed to its operational area by a mother ship. The USS *Dolphin* (AGSS 55) is the navy's only diesel-electric deep-diving submersible and is used for equipment evaluation, oceanic surveys, and weapons trials. Primarily used to test new technologies, the *Dolphin* can carry up to 12 tons of equipment. It is based at San Diego and although essentially a naval vessel, it has also been used by civilian and scientific researchers. The LSV 2 (Large Scale Vehicle 2) was named USS *Cutthroat* in November 2000, and is an unmanned submersible that is chiefly a test bed for submarine technologies. Among the research that has been conducted are stealth, hydrodynamics, hydroacoustics, and propulsion systems that might be fitted into future U.S. Navy submarines. It is based at the Acoustic Research Detachment in Bayview, Idaho, and operates on Lake Pend Oreille under the immediate direction of the Naval Warfare Center's Carderock Division. The *Sea Sparrow* is a surface ship that grew out of a collaboration between the navy, the Advanced Research Projects Agency and Lockheed Martin Missiles and Space Company. A twin-hulled design, it has stealth characteristics and is used to test cutting-edge technologies, such as control, automation, and sea-keeping systems.

Data: USS *Dolphin* AGSS 555
Length: 165 feet
Displacement: 950 tons (full load)
Diving depth: 3,000 feet
Crew: 5 officers; 46 other ranks; up to 5 scientists
Date Deployed: August 17, 1968

Data: LSV 2—Large Scale Vehicle 2)
Length: 111 feet
Displacement: 205 tons

Data: Sea Shadow)Length: 164 feet
Displacement: 560 tons (full load)
Crew: 10 officers and other ranks.

Data: NR 1 Deep Submergence Craft
Length: 567 feet
Displacement: 400 tons.
Speed: Four knots (submerged).
Diving depth: 2,375 feet
Crew: 2 officers; 3 other ranks; 2 scientists.
Armament: Date deployed: October 27, 1969.

Hall of Fame

All of the world's major navies revere their traditions and heritage and many have taken positive steps to preserve some of their most important warships from the past. The U.S. Navy is no different in this respect and has kept in commission or donated as museums to public bodies some of its most significant vessels from both the distant and recent past. In the former case is the USS *Constitution*, a frigate from the first days of the United States that narrowly avoided the breakers' yard on several occasions, while in the latter category are the four battleships of the mighty Iowa class that first saw service during World War II and last put to sea in anger during the late 1990s.

THIS PAGE AND RIGHT: USS *Constitution* ("Old Ironsides"), the oldest commissioned warship afloat, makes her annual 4th of July turnaround cruise in Boston Harbor. USS *Constitution's* cannons were among the most powerful to set sail on any warship in her day.
U.S. Navy photos by Journalist Seaman Joe Burgess (this page) and Photographer's Mate 1st Class Alexander C. Hicks J. (right)

FAR RIGHT: U.S. Navy Commander Michael Beck and his crew man the sides of the USS *Constitution.*
U.S. Navy photo by Photographer's Mate 1st Class Alexander C. Hicks Jr.

USS *Constitution*

The USS *Constitution*, a three-mast frigate affectionately nicknamed "Old Ironsides," is the oldest commissioned warship in the world still afloat. Its career began after Congress passed an act in March 1794 to expand the U.S. Navy. This led to a design by Joshua Humphreys, who created a wooden warship that was larger and more heavily armed than conventional frigates. Construction work was undertaken at Edmond Hart's Shipyard in Boston, Massachusetts, and cost some $302,000 at the time. Paul Revere forged the copper spikes and bolts that held its planking in position as well as the copper sheathing that covered the hull. First deployed in October 1797, the *Constitution* put to sea in July of the following year and saw service in the War against France. In 1803 she was made the flagship of Captain Edward Preble's U.S. Mediterranean squadron, and fought in the wars against the Barbary pirates of North Africa. During the War of 1812 against Britain, the *Constitution* under Captain Isaac Hull took on the Royal Navy's *Guerriere* in the Gulf of St. Lawrence. In 30 minutes the British warship was left as little more than a hulk while the *Constitution* suffered virtually no damage. British cannonballs mostly bounced off her sides and the ship thus earned its nickname. The *Constitution* was found unserviceable in 1830 but was saved from scrapping in part due to a poem, "Old Ironsides," penned by Oliver Wendell Holmes. Full decommission came in 1882 but she was once again saved from demolition and in 1925 underwent restoration paid for by public donation. Recommissioned in 1932, the frigate was placed in permanent commission in 1941 and since 1954 the Secretary of the Navy has been wholly responsible for the *Constitution*'s upkeep.

Length: 204 feet

Displacement: 2,200 tons

Powerplant: 42,710 square feet of sail on fore, main, and mizzen-masts

Speed: 13+ knots

Crew: 450 including a 55-strong detachment of Marines (1797)

Armament: 32 x 24 lb long-range cannon; 20 x 32 lb carronades; 2 x 24 lb bow-chasers

LEFT: Off the coast of Massachusetts a modern sailor "mans the rail" from on board the U.S. Navy destroyer USS *Ramage* (DDG 61). *Constitution* was commissioned on October 21, 1797.
U.S. Navy photo by Chief Photographer John E. Gay

Iowa class

By the spring of 1958 the U.S. Navy had dispensed with
its last battleships viewing them as redundant in the face
of more powerful submarines and aircraft carriers and
unsuited to the realities of the ongoing Cold War.
However, several of the Iowa class, which had been built
during World War II, were destined to serve again until
the early 1990s. The USS *New Jersey* (BB 62) was briefly
recommissioned in the early Vietnam War but was taken
out of service in 1969. However, the battleship again
returned to service in 1982, not only equipped with the
usual 16-inch guns but also Harpoon anti-ship missiles
and Tomahawk cruise missiles. From May 1984, as the
U.S. Navy was endeavoring to reach a strength of 600
warships of all types, the other Iowa class battleships
were also taken out of mothballs and underwent a
modernization program. However, cost-cutting exercises
soon sealed their fate; the *Iowa* (BB 61) and *New Jersey*
were decommissioned in early 1991, although the other
two battleships in the class, the *Missouri* (BB 63) and
Wisconsin (BB 64), enjoyed a stay of execution to take
part in 1991's Operation Desert Storm. Following
the conclusion of hostilities, the *Wisconsin* was
decommissioned in September 1991 and the *Missouri*
suffered a similar fate on March 31, 1992. Today they
are all still afloat as museums: BB 61 at Suisan Bay, San
Francisco, California, BB 62 at Camden, New Jersey,
BB 63 at Pearl Harbor, Hawaii, and BB 64 at Norfolk,
Virginia.

Data: Iowa 1943
Length: 887 feet 3 inches
Displacement: 57,600 tons (full load)
Speed: 33 knots
Crew: 2,800 officers and other ranks
Armament: Nine sixteen-inch guns in three turrets;
20 five-inch DP guns; 60 x 40 mm AAA guns; 60 x 20
mm AAA guns

LEFT: The battleship USS *Wisconsin* (BB 64) fires her sixteen-inch guns during a 1980s exercise.
U.S. Navy photo

LEFT: The battleship USS *Missouri* (BB 63) passes Diamond Head en route to Pearl Harbor, Hawaii.
U.S. Navy photo by Photographer's Mate 2nd Class Kerry E. Baker

LEFT: The battleship USS *New Jersey* (BB 62) fires a volley of sixteen inch shells while off the coast of Japan during a training exercise. *New Jersey* is followed by the USS *Missouri* (BB 63), the nuclear-powered guided missile cruiser USS *Long Beach* (CGN 9), and other units of the Third Fleet—a 1990s view.
U.S. Navy file photo

RIGHT: The battleship *Missouri* (BB 63) "Mighty Mo"—ties up to its new pier at Ford Island in Pearl Harbor, Hawaii. The USS *Arizona* Memorial is in the background.
U.S. Navy photo by Photographer's Mate 2nd Class Kerry Baker

ABOVE: As the aircraft carrier USS *Carl Vinson* (CVN 70) pulls into Pearl Harbor, the crew
render honors to battleship USS *Missouri* (BB 63).
U.S. Navy photo by Photographer's Mate 3rd Class Christopher Hollaway

SEAPOWER | HALL OF FAME

ABOVE LEFT: Another view of USS *Wisconsin* (BB 64) on her final voyage.
U.S. Navy photo by Journalist 3rd Class David Valdez

LEFT AND ABOVE: The battleship *Missouri* (BB 63) "Mighty Mo" enters Pearl Harbor en route to its new berth at Ford Island near the USS *Arizona* Memorial. Secretary of the Navy John H. Dalton signed the Donation Agreement on May 4, 1998, allowing *Missouri* to be used as a museum near the Arizona Memorial.
U.S. Navy photo by Photographer's Mate 2nd Class Kerry Baker

RIGHT: Sailors and Marines aboard the amphibious assault ship USS *Peleliu* (LHA 5) render honors to the USS *Arizona* Memorial and the battleship *Missouri*.
U.S. Navy photo by Photographer's Mate 1st Class William R. Goodwin

Glossary

AAV	Amphibious assault vehicle
AAAV	Advanced amphibious assault vehicle
AAW	Anti-air warfare
ACV	Air cushion vehicle
AE	Ammunition ship
AFG	Command ship
AH	Hospital ship
AOE	Fast combat support ship
ARG	Amphibious ready group
ARM	Anti-radiation missile
ARS	Rescue and salvage ship
AS	Submarine tender
ASROC	Anti-submarine missile
ASM	Air-to-surface missile
ASW	Anti-submarine warfare
ATF	Amphibious task force
BPDMS	Base point defense missile system
CG	Guided missile cruiser
CIWS	Close-in weapons system
CVSG	Carrier strike group
CV	Conventionally powered aircraft carrier
CVBG	Carrier battle group
CVN	Nuclear-powered aircraft carrier
DD	Destroyer
DDG	Guided missile destroyer
DSV	Deep submergence vehicle
DSRV	Deep submergence rescue vehicle
ECM	Electronic countermeasures
Elint	Electronic intelligence
EW	Electronic warfare
FOD	Foreign objects debris
FFG	Guided missile frigate
GFCS	Gunfire control system
GMLS	Guided missile launch system
GRP	Glass-reinforced plastic fiberglass

GWS	Guided weapons system
LAMPS	Light airborne multi-purpose system (helicopter)
LAMS	Local area missile system
LCAC	Landing craft air cushion
LCM	Landing craft mechanized
LCU	Landing craft utility
LCVP	Landing craft vehicle personnel
LHA	Helicopter assault ship
LHD	Helicopter dock assault
LPD	Amphibious transport dock
LSD	Dock landing ship
LSV	Large scale vehicle
MCM	Mine countermeasures ship
MEU	Marine expeditionary unit
MFCS	Missile fire control system
MHC	Coastal minehunter

MIDAS	Mine and ice detection and avoidance system
MSC	Minesweeper coastal
MSC	Military Sealift Command
PC	Patrol craft
PDMS	Point defense missile system
RAM	Rolling airframe missile
RHIB	Rigid hull inflatable boat
ROV	Remotely operated vehicle
SAM	Surface-to-air missile
SAR	Search and rescue
SEAL	SEa Air Land
SLCM	Submarine-launched cruise missile
SLEP	Service life extension program
SOC	Special operations craft

SSBN	Nuclear ballistic missile submarine
SSGN	Nuclear guided missile submarine
SSM	Surface-to-surface missile
SSN	Nuclear attack submarine
SSTDS	Surface ship torpedo detection system
TASM	Tomahawk antiship missile
TLAM	Tomahawk land-attack missile (high-explosive warhead)
TLAM–N	Tomahawk land-attack missile (nuclear warhead)
VERTREP	Vertical replenishment
VFA	Strike fighter squadron (eg VFA-86)
VLA	Vertical launch ASROC
YP	Yard patrol craft